"This book is a scientifically well researched ... help you and your child thrive. Every perso... our children's future should ...

Dr Maria Isaac, Tenured Professor of ... Psychological Medicine, University of London

"Wabi-sabi is the powerful Japanese aesthetic centred on the acceptance of imperfection and transience. Imagine if every child was taught to realise this principle; what a magnificent and purposeful future for humanity. This is the central premise of "How to Thrive by Building Resilience." Belen captures empathy, love, life and every child reaching their fullest potential."

Nandini, CEO, Procurement Leaders, Mother of one

"It is rare to find such a helpful book written so intelligently with principles you can actually apply."

Myrto C, M&A Lawyer, Mother of two

"Although I am used to deliver under pressure and I feel happy and engaged in what I do, as a father I did not know how to start talking to my son about these important aspects. Despite the book not belonging to my usual reading genre, It has proven to be an easy to- use roadmap to explore, discuss and consciously educate our family to make the most of the opportunities life brings."

Yago, CEO, Zens Group, Father of one

"A truly inspirational book that every parent should own."

Florence, Stay At Home Mother of two

"This book gives me inspiration to be a better parent for my girls in this very challenging world."

Sarah, Stay At Home Mother of two

"I already feel like it is making a difference in my personal life and having a positive impact on the children."

Headteacher, Mother of two

HOW TO
THRIVE
BY BUILDING
RESILIENCE

A guide for you and your child

BELEN DEL AMO PEREZ DE LARA

A 3VERS Publication

To my parents, as they were exemplars of loving and resilient parenting, making me the person that I am today.
May they rest in peace.

To my husband, for he gave meaning to my life when I lost my best friend, only to find a lifelong one in him, and much more.

To my kids, for they gave meaning to my life when I became an adult orphan, transforming me into a mother, and helping me become a better version of myself.

To the dear friends that believed in me when I struggled to believe in myself.

Contents

Introduction: What is Resilience?

Resilience, defined as the ability to positively adapt to an adverse situation,[1] enables higher levels of individual performance and well-being. Resilience is key for good mental health, as it not only provides a buffer against psychological pressures, but it also helps us be at our best when it matters most, and sustain our best over time. Research has shown that children first learn resilience skills from their parents and primary caretakers, mirroring the way we react to setbacks, stress, change, and uncertainty. Clearly, we need to be as thoughtful in developing our children's resilience as we are deliberate in helping them learn their maths.

I believe the combination of examinations, an educational system that often extols competition, and parental focus on breeding 'successful children' that 'win' in high-pressured environments, is a huge part of the reason we perceive a rise in mental health issues around us today. While mental health problems have been around since long before our time, and there is mixed evidence as to whether they are in fact rising or not, there is a definite shift in the way we are coping with them, given the exacerbated demands on our time due to social media, digitisation, and other societal changes.

Mental health problems are one of the main causes of the overall disease burden worldwide. One in six people suffer or have suffered from psychological issues, 50% of which arise

---

[1] Masten, Cutuli, Herbers, and Reed, 2009.

before the age of fifteen, and 75% before a child's eighteenth birthday. Suicide has become the biggest killer of young people in the UK. Movements to call for more mental health awareness, and the reduction of stigma associated to it, are springing up everywhere you look, yet in spite of research being conducted, less than 30% of it is focused on young people. Of course, exams, competition, high-pressured environments, and stress are part of life, and something all our children will encounter. So how can we best prepare them to 'bounce back', better and stronger, and even thrive while doing so?

While resilience comes naturally to some, fortunately it is a skill that can be learnt, and learnt at any age. With this book, my mission is to provide a pragmatic, empathic, and scientifically grounded approach to raising thriving children, while at the same time sharing some tips to help their parents thrive too.

How to thrive by building resilience

Resilience is part of the broader field of positive psychology, the scientific study of human flourishing. In other words, positive psychology is the study of how each of us can live our best life, and resilience is one of the skills that enables that. When co-founding the global leadership coaching firm, Perez Fitzgerald, and later founding 3VERS,[2] a company that helps executives, parents, and educators develop resilience, I took a slightly broader approach. Leveraging leading insights from neuroscience, positive psychology, and the C-suite,[3] I chose to define resilience as the *ability to adapt and sustain the best version of ourselves in order to thrive*. My aim was to highlight that it is not just about what we do when times are tough, it is also about what we do when times go well, that will help us thrive.

By developing this resilience toolkit, our children will be best equipped to deal with the pressures of life and find their true

---

[2] Pronounced 'Thrivers'.

[3] This term refers to individuals reporting to the Chief Executive Officer (CEO), or one level below.

calling. While some may define success as reaching the higher echelons of leadership, others may define it as something entirely different, but the elements required to reach success, **in a healthy, sustainable manner**, are what we will discuss in this book under the term 'resilience'.

As technology marches forward, the established phases of human life – education, higher education, career, and retirement – are likely to merge. That will be exciting, yet also unsettling. Instead of a career for life, those in school now are predicted to have had ten different jobs by the time they are forty. Chances are they'll be freelancers, picking up tasks outsourced by companies across the globe, managing their own financial affairs beyond the safety blanket of a monthly pay cheque. The advances of AI and other technologies may significantly reduce the number of jobs available to them.

Our principal role as parents today is to prepare our children for that uncertainty. To foster in them the confidence, drive, and resilience – mental and physical – for a world in which bespoke solutions to boost their talents will exist, if only they are persistent enough to seek them out.

Resilience is the key skill in dealing with uncertainty

Today's educational systems are primarily designed to teach our children to acquire knowledge in maths, grammar, science, and other disciplines, which are frequently taught separately from one another. The system is structured to measure success through regular exams and rankings, with top spots earned when pupils outwork or outsmart the competition. Yet when children leave education, they are expected to create work of value, as opposed to regurgitating knowledge; collaborate by working in groups, as opposed to competing against one another; and think critically to solve problems – not to learn subjects and showcase their knowledge for the sake of an exam mark. Most schools aren't yet equipped to teach resilience as deliberately and thoughtfully as they do these other subjects. It is hard not to feel that our children's emotional education, ability to adapt to change, critical thinking, and ability to thrive in ambiguity is left up to either the benevolence or genius of a particular teacher, or to us, the parents.

For parents willing and able to micromanage children's routes to 'success', the importance of building resilience, therefore, ought to serve as something of a warning. We have to stop doing everything for them: stop the endless stimuli so they are never bored and never have to work out what to do next for themselves; stop hovering so they never graze their knees if they fall; resist the urge to leap in and show them the right answers. Instead, let them play games of their own devising, let them fail, and let them fail repeatedly. We need to stop defining success for them with the old archetypes we were born into, and instead empower them to set their own goals, identify their own strengths and motivations, and give them the tools to pursue those relentlessly, with passion. We need to stop falling victim to peer pressure or the pressures of the educational system, that can take our children to the point of burn-out, compromising their childhoods and setting them up for perilous journeys to 'empty success', plagued with feelings of inadequacy and lack of fulfilment.

With the assistance of neuroscience and positive psychology, I will guide you through the most pragmatic research out there so that you can both build resilience yourself, and pass the tools down to your child. This will enable you to confidently lead yourself and your child through the unexpected, so that they can do more than 'succeed': I want to empower you to help them *thrive*.

Neuroscience, Positive Psychology, and the PERMA(S) model

What is neuroscience?

Emerging in the 20th century, the fast-growing field of neuroscience is the study of the brain, and has witnessed significant breakthroughs in recent years. At 1.3 kg in weight, the human brain consists of many nerve cells. The latter, called neurons, connect to create a network of interlinking circuits. These circuits in the brain are responsible for our 'thoughts, mood, emotions, intelligence, as well as our physical movement, breathing, heart rate, and sleep.' The brain regulates and is responsible for almost every aspect of what it means to be alive.[4]

Mirror neurons found in the brain fire not only when you perform an action, but also when you *observe* someone performing an action, meaning that while watching us as parents respond to adversity, change, and the unknown, our children's brains are sculpting neural pathways that they will draw upon themselves as they progress through life.

Before you worry that this book will be overly technical, let me assure you that we will discuss practical applications of neuroscience as a means to grow in self-awareness and in

---

[4] The British Neuroscience Association, https://www.bna.org.uk/about-neuroscience/

developing our children's.

What is positive psychology?

While traditional psychology focuses on treating diagnosed mental illness, positive psychology – the scientific study of human flourishing – deliberately promotes mental wellness. Martin Seligman and his fellow positive psychologists each contributed various strands of thinking to the field, including Seligman's own PERMA model, which encompasses the main components of a happy, thriving life. According to Seligman's research, introduced in his 2011 publication, *Flourish: A Visionary New Understanding of Happiness and Well-being,* the presence of the following acronym helps a person be their best self, and these attributes can be found amongst top performers in many fields (at least on their way up):

Positive emotions

How often and how intensely do you experience positive emotions? This category is broader than just happiness, and includes joy, gratitude, contentment, pride, love, serenity, interest, and hope. The aim with this dimension of human flourishing is to experience a range of emotions, with a slight slant towards generating more positive than negative emotions and to experience positive emotions more intensely than negative ones *over time.* The good news is that we can control this, and we will learn how.

Engagement

How often do you feel like time flies by because you are so deeply engaged in doing something that you lose track of everything else? Psychologists call this reaching a 'state of flow', where we are sufficiently stretched yet not overly so, and are at our best. Seligman proposes that using our strengths daily can enhance our experience of flow, and that this state is essential for our human flourishing.

Relationships

Do you have that person to call at 3.00 am if there is an emergency? How intimate are your relationships? There do not have to be many, but the presence of at least one close relationship is crucial for our well-being, confidence, and as we will later see, health and longevity.

Meaning

Do you have a higher purpose? Or do you lead a spiritual life? How you connect your life with the bigger picture – across time, space, and the self – determines how much meaning you experience in your life. People with a clear meaning or purpose tend to experience more positive emotions across time, and ultimately lead healthier and longer lives.

Achievement

When do you feel most accomplished, and how often? Seligman argues that accomplishment is something people seek even in the absence of other aspects of a full life, such as positive emotion, engagement, and meaning. Whether it is truly separable is an ongoing matter for debate amongst psychologists. That said, it is closely linked to goal pursuit in particular. We will define it as setting a goal and accomplishing it.

I would like to add one more category into the mix:

Self-Acceptance

According to Seligman, if you actively pay attention to building and maintaining the five aspects of the PERMA model, you will flourish. However, my experience coaching high-performing individuals across the corporate world showed me that this might not be enough to *sustain* performance across time. Many outwardly 'successful' clients confessed private feelings of inadequacy and unhappiness, as they felt they could always do more at the expense of their well-being.

Furthermore, imposter syndrome, an overinflated sense of doubt that can lead to high levels of anxiety, will be experienced by roughly 70% of people. This syndrome isn't uncommon amongst high performers across various fields, and it is easy to see how the feelings could originate and manifest in childhood.

As such, there is merit in adding a separate 'S' component to the PERMA model with **Self-acceptance**,[5] to raise awareness of the importance to accept ourselves just as we are. Maybe we don't want to be C-suite executives and instead want to be world-class musicians? Maybe we don't want to lead big teams and instead want to work alone? Maybe we would rather spend time playing outside with our friends than being tutored in a subject we hate, and which is causing us stress? Sometimes it is critical for our mental health to accept our limits for what they are, learn to live with them, and move on.

Finding the balance between our best performance and our well-being should be powered by a healthy understanding of ourselves and our needs. Being raised in a household where parents/caretakers label you as 'not good enough', 'lazy', or 'naughty', can also translate into a harsh inner script that fosters an overly self-critical adult. But how helpful is it to be self-critical to the point of pessimism, anxiety, and self-loathing?

You are the one person you will spend the most time with across your lifetime. Thus taking care of you and turning those internal niggles into helpful, kind, and positive thoughts, can be the greatest gift you give yourself, and in turn, your child.

---

[5] Shepard (1979), defines it as an individual's satisfaction or happiness with oneself, and is considered necessary for good mental health.

Want to check in with yourself? How present on a scale from one to ten do you think these are for you? And for your child?

Positive Emotions		
Engagement		
Relationships		
Meaning		
Accomplishment		
Self-Acceptance		

The 3VERS Journey: How to Use this Book

If it hasn't become apparent yet, human flourishing can be learnt, and I aim to give you practical tools to help you nurture this methodology within yourself, and in turn, help your child develop the skills from an early age. This book goes beyond helping you get closer to PERMAS: it will introduce the most helpful and pragmatic insights from neuroscience, positive psychology, and the C-suite that you can use to develop the skills independently and thrive with confidence. In other words, you won't need the assistance of a coach or therapist, unless you choose to engage in such support to rewire bad habits.

Once you've created good habits for yourself, you can then teach them to your child through modelling or more formal transmission. I have included a number of exercises to perform alone and with your child, lasting from ten minutes to two weeks in duration. Some exercises may need to be slightly adapted to suit your child's age. You may find that you use many of the techniques outlined in this book already, in which case, my hope is that you will go from unconscious competence to conscious competence (more on this later), so that you can teach others to be as resilient as you already are. The book will give you a space to reflect on how to do the latter with your children.

I have organised resilience-building into four distinct parts. Each section builds upon the other, giving us the opportunity to consolidate strategies as we move from one to the next. I have also found that people benefit from information-chunking into a logical journey, making the insights easier to absorb, apply, and relate to.

1. **Aligning Life** – This section will help us identify what really matters to us, and align our life to achieve those things. We will look at the science of high performance and what it has to say about motivation, goal-setting, and goal alignment. The section will help us develop our achievement and meaning (PERMA**S**.) We will learn to organise our goals in ways that they support one another so as to reach persistence and coherence of motive – proven to correlate directly with success in whatever field you pursue. We will then focus on how to teach these skills to your children by breaking it down to the simplest of forms: goal formation, problem resolution, and the appreciation that there are many ways to reach your ultimate goal, helping us build more flexibility into our lives and as a consequence, a more resilient approach towards goal pursuit.

2. **Aligning Mindsets** – This section will lay the foundations to create an agile, resilient mindset that more closely aligns to the reality of the situations we face. The insights from this section will help us absorb the tools and techniques that I will share in Sections III and IV. It will develop our positive emotions, self-acceptance, achievement, meaning, and relationships (**PERMAS**). Together, we will understand why having a growth and stress-is-enhancing mindset can power our performance. We will learn the basics of neuroscience to understand what happens inside our brain when we get stressed, and some simple hacks to manage that. All of this will be presented in a simplified, child-friendly, yet evidence-based way, so that you can transmit these

concepts to your children. The idea is that you and your child will have a common language to explain what is happening when we are stressed or under pressure, whilst maintaining a calm and resilient mindset to deal with it.

3. **Building Reactive Resilience** – This section will introduce the concept of explanatory style to convey the importance of mentally robust ways to respond to negative events. It will develop a more balanced and realistic set of emotions, and help us build relationships, and in particular self-acceptance (**PERMAS**). This section will require that you (a) do a lot of self-analysis, and (b) practise the tools on yourself first, then (c) teach the tools to your children. We will dedicate parts of this section to explain how you can convey the basics of these tools, including generating higher-level thinking skills, identifying alternative ways to explain a problem, exploring ways to seek evidence, and raising awareness of simple mental cognitive distortions your child may be falling victim to.

4. **Building Proactive Resilience** – This section will identify the applications of how generating positive emotion, and the various tools to achieve it, can help us lead a more fulfilling life, and lift the performance of others around us. It will bring together every aspect of PERMAS and build upon the work in previous sections. As with every other section, there will be a space for you to think about how to incorporate these habits into your own life and your child's routine.

In summary, this book will show that future success is entirely compatible with well-being if we apply knowledge from across various fields to help us get there. More importantly, it will give you the knowledge, tools, and time to *reflect*, so you can enable your child to build resilience in order to thrive.

Let's get started.

Section I

Aligning Life

I'd love to share an excerpt with you from a book I have written for my children to read when they are older.

Love ... love for my mother is something that I find difficult to explain. It is all encompassing and reassuring: the feeling of being wrapped up in a warm blanket that smells of your favourite scent, getting cuddles from the person that knows you best, and having all the reassurance in the world that everything will be okay. She was the force behind my optimism and my belief that I could do anything I set my mind to. That no matter how tough times got (and in all fairness, we were lucky), I could do anything. That the future was always bright, with new adventures to look forward to. That things always worked out in the end. Until I lost her to cancer.

I had to rebuild everything from within. My identity, my confidence, my hopes, my dreams. I had to come to terms with the fact that my life up to this point had led me to be very close to my mom, slightly less so to my dad, and that I had no real lifelong friends. I felt terribly alone. For an extrovert who was used to being around a lot of people, it was a tough pill to swallow – to realise the people you thought were friends, were merely people with whom you shared a period of your life. To realise that you only knew your father through your mother's eyes or in your mother's company. That life was more than going to an Ivy League University, graduating top of your class, working at JP Morgan, living in a beautiful house in Notting Hill, and going out to the best bars and clubs. That this 'perfect trajectory' meant absolutely nothing. That the only thing that really matters is what and whom you leave behind once you are gone.

The people you leave behind are those that keep you alive through their memories, and the spoken or written word. The impact you leave behind is what drives people to speak of you and remember you fondly. That is all that truly matters – finding your people, finding your passion, sharing it with people to impact their lives for the good. When my mother died, I realised that the most important thing for me was family, and that now 50% of mine was gone forever. I had to rebuild.

When I was nineteen, my mother was diagnosed with a rare type of terminal cancer, which few doctors knew much about. I was an only child and had grown up moving around my entire life, from city to city and country to country. I had lived in twenty-one different cities by the time I was twenty-four, rebuilding a life each time, knowing there was finite time to do it and considerable pressure to do it well. My father, a successful, driven, hardworking, and passionate businessman, raised me to believe I was meant to be CEO of General Electric one day. And my mother, who with her intellect and skills was unable to work because of the frequency of our moves, was the most devoted of stay-at-home moms, indelibly leaving a vision of motherhood in my mind that I would later need to reconcile. Right before she died, when I was twenty-one, my view on life was simple: my job was to do my best day in and day out, and aim high for the top, the absolute top – top of my class, top university, top blue chip employer. The rest would become clearer as I progressed, but I felt I had lots to look forward to.

All this was turned on its head when I saw what actually

happens after a person dies. It propelled me to ask myself a lot of questions. If an upward career to become CEO of JP Morgan (where I was working at the time) wasn't the goal, what was? The answer to this question, which I took another ten years to be able to answer following my father's death to cancer, forms the basic framework for a resilient life, and although our intermediate and short-term goals will shift across time, their essence can be accessed if only we ask ourselves the right questions and are brave enough to listen to the answers.

1 | Defining Success and Aligning Goals

If I asked you if the Dalai Lama is 'successful', what would you say? What about Richard Branson/Donald Trump/Sheryl Sandberg? Your doctor/lawyer/teacher friend? If I asked them if they thought of themselves as successful, what do you think they would say?

Success means different things to different people. For some it may be to be the wealthiest person in the world; for others it may be to have a happy, healthy family; yet others may have a different wish – to live according to their values and be content with what they have.

Whatever your definition of success, the main task is to outline any smaller goals that support the larger goal, so we can sustain the good habits that drive motivation and outcomes. Indeed, how you define success is a key contributing factor to how likely you will be able to sustain your motive and actions, and thus enhance the likelihood that you will achieve what you first set out to do.

Some of the world's most successful people have simply figured out how to align their values, their aspirations, and their strengths with their overall life set-up, so they can exhibit and work towards what Angela Duckworth elegantly describes in her book *Grit: The Power of Passion and Perseverance*, as 'persistence and coherence of motive'. Her research shows that, to be at the top of any field, besides natural ability – after all, no matter how much determination we have, we can't all be Usain Bolt – we also need persistence of motive. It is this that will allow us to sustain the habits that differentiate us from the rest, whether those entail early-morning training sessions, conducting extra research, or sticking to our guns.

We need to develop the ability to pursue the same ultimate goal day in, day out, year in, year out. While this main goal is often the result of years – or even a lifetime – of work, it matters enough to top performers that they always keep it in view. And while there are countless milestones to achieve along the way, top performers do not confuse these intermediate goals with the real thing. They know how to prioritise, because they are clear on the difference between the means and the end. And they trade everything else out.

We often have too many goals, and as a result we lose focus. We feel overwhelmed and we struggle to prioritise – especially when our goals appear to be in conflict. Furthermore, when we have so many apparently competing goals, we are disappointed when we fail to achieve them all. This disappointment can lead us to become demotivated and feel like we are incapable of following through on the behaviours necessary to achieve what is most important. Our daily frustrations – our underperformance compared to the goals we set ourselves – become evidence that maybe we do not have what it takes.

So how do we fix that? How do we first define what success looks like to us in order to find this persistence of motive, and then feed it back down to your child? Well, this may entail you, personally, going back to the drawing board.

You may be one of the lucky ones that knew exactly what you wanted to do from a young age, in which case you're probably already living a pretty good life. You may find, however, that the desire to do one thing side-tracked you from other things that were also important.

Alternatively, you may not have known what you wanted to do, but had parents who, in thinking they worked in your interest, nudged you in the 'right' direction. Now you find yourself in a job that isn't necessarily aligned to your natural preferences or innate personality traits. Worse yet, as with around 70% of the population, you may feel like an imposter in your chosen area of work. Neuroscience teaches us that doing things that align more neatly to our preferences (or more established neural pathways – more on this later) requires less energy. Thus attempting to align our life activities to those preferences leaves us more energy for other things (including more energy to pursue our goals day in, day out).

You may feel your life is just where you want it to be. In that case, either you lucked out or you knew yourself so well that you knew what you loved and organised the entirety of your life to doing that, whilst fitting in the things that are important to you. This does not mean you did not have to make hard trade-offs. In fact, it probably means you made loads of them. In my book, that is the true definition of success: identifying what you love, doing what you love (hoping it helps others too), and being content with what you have, with the confidence to say no to the things that do not fit. So if you're not one of those lucky ones, how do you start? Top down or bottom up?

The answer to that depends hugely on your thinking style. If you're a **macro** person (big ideas first, then drill down to the details), you may prefer to start asking yourself the hard questions, then work backwards. If you lead a strong spiritual life, this may be easy for you to do. Alternatively, you may be a **micro** person (details first before you build the big picture) and may thus prefer to work backwards, and identify your lower level goals to build a goal hierarchy.[6] So let's have a go at the two approaches and see which one suits you best, by filling in the boxes below.

[6] Robinson and Moeller, 2014.

Exercise I: Macro to Micro Goal Formation

Self-Reflection: How do I define success?

If, after a lot of self-analysis and soul-searching, you're still struggling to answer this question in a way that feels authentic to you, you may want to try an exercise that one of my INSEAD professors asked us to do during one of her brilliant classes in Singapore. She asked us to write down how we would like someone to describe us in two to three paragraphs, if they were writing an article about us towards the end of our life. What you choose to write will undoubtedly reveal the things you care about most, and hopefully the things that will feature at the very top of your goal hierarchy (which we will explore during the next exercise).

Self-Reflection: What does my child's success look like?

The above is another way to articulate how you will know when your child is 'successful'. What are the markers? Because these are the markers you are subconsciously and/or consciously transmitting to them. Becoming aware of them can help you realise if what you are transmitting is what you want to transmit. It will also allow you to later confirm whether your child is interpreting these markers as you intend. For example, my parents may have just wanted me to be happy, but for a long time I thought they wanted me to get into an Ivy League School to make them proud. It is only with hindsight that I realise the assumption they were making was that going to an Ivy League would make *me* happier in the long run.

Discussion: How does my child define success? How do they think I define it?

Whilst the discussion will depend on your child's age, and the relationship you share, notice the differences between your child's definition of success and your own goals and definition of their success. Although as parents we often want the best for our kids, we tend to project our own goals onto them, forgetting that they are human beings in the making, with their own developing preferences and skills. Recognising the difference between our desires and helping our children identify their own is the first step to ensuring your child can build that innate persistence of motive through intrinsic rather than extrinsic motivation.

If you found the macro to micro exercise helpful, wonderful. If not, then let's see if Exercise II is more aligned to your learning style. Most people can benefit from completing a goal hierarchy exercise to crystallise their goals, align their life – what we often think of as work-life balance is actually just an alignment of all the things we love – and find reassurance that they're going in the right direction.

What is a goal hierarchy?[7]

Goal hierarchies offer a way for us to cut through the noise of countless objectives, to focus on what's important, and to sustain motivation even when we encounter failure and disappointment.

We all have things that we want to achieve on any given day, week, and month. But not all goals are equal. Some goals are the *means* and some are the *ends*. For example, we may have many concrete lower-level goals (e.g. make a nutritious lunch from scratch for my kids, make five important work calls, go to HIIT class), but these are serving intermediate-level goals (e.g. healthy eating for the family, grow my business, reduce my body fat), that are, in turn, serving our highest-level goals (e.g. help my kids thrive, create financial independence so I can take care of my family, stay healthy so that I can enjoy life to the full). The lower-level goals are the *means* and the higher-level goals are the *ends* – the ones we really care about.

As I've mentioned before, outstanding entrepreneurs and athletes have been characterised by what has been termed 'persistence of motive': they pursue the same ultimate goal, day in, day out, year in, year out. This does not mean that they have the same lower level goals each day, week, or month. Indeed, their lower-level goals may change frequently. But it does mean they consistently pursue a clear over-arching goal, such as 'being the best in my field' or 'building a global business' or 'providing a loving and comfortable home environment'. Having a clear sense of their ultimate motive makes it easier for these resilient individuals to sustain the behaviours needed for them to achieve their lower-level goals; prioritise between alternative, competing lower-level goals; and bounce back from failures in pursuit of lower-level goals, because their higher-level goals remain intact and they can 're-goal' by identifying alternative means to their ultimate 'ends'.

---

[7] What follows in this goal hierarchy section is an exercise inspired by positive psychologists, and developed at Perez Fitzgerald.

Exercise II: Micro to Macro Goal Formation

Step 1: List your goals

Take five minutes to list all the goals you can think of for the next day, week and month. These can include both concrete and abstract goals. The resulting list should give you a good sense of the goals that direct your attention.

#	Goals
1	
2	
3	
4	
5	
6	
7	
8	
9	
10	
11	
12	
13	
14	
15	
16	
17	
18	
19	
20	

Step 2: Craft your goal hierarchy

An easy way to sketch out a goal-hierarchy is to categorise goals into three groups: high-level (ends), intermediate-level (means), and low-level (means). See the following example:

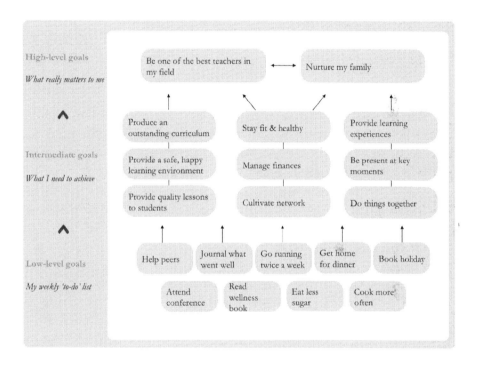

1. Use the 'My Goal Hierarchy' space below to articulate your higher-level goal(s). You may frame this as the main purpose of your professional or personal life, or you may choose to articulate two higher-level goals (one that encapsulates your professional aspirations and one for your personal aspirations). If you choose this option, you may want to reflect on how you can craft your two higher-level goals so that they are *supportive* of each other, rather than *competing* with each other.

2. Once you have articulated your higher-level goal(s), incorporate the goals you identified in Step 1 into your goal-hierarchy diagram, with the most concrete, least important goals at the lower-level, and the more important goals at the intermediate-level.

3. Once you have completed your sketch, reflect individually on the following questions:

- To what extent do your identified lower/intermediate-level goals ('means') support what matters to you ('ends')?

- Are there some lower-level goals that are not contributing to your higher-level goals at all? If so, is this because there is a higher-level goal that you have not articulated, or are these lower-level goals merely a wasteful distraction?

- Now that you have made your higher-level goal(s) explicit, are there any additional mid- or lower-level goals that you would insert in your sketch?

- Just as importantly, which goals should you abandon or adapt – either because they are not helping you drive towards what matters most to you, or because they are taking disproportionate time and energy that could be better spent on other lower/intermediate-level goals ('means')?

My Goal Hierarchy

High-level goals

What really matters to me

∧

Intermediate goals

What I need to achieve

∧

Low-level goals

My weekly 'to-do' list

Whether you completed your goal hierarchy or preferred the macro to micro approach, take a look now at your higher-level goals. What is the motivation behind them? Motivation is defined as 'why people do what they do', so if you don't know the motivation behind your top level goals it, is important that you ask yourself 'why is this goal important to me?' The reason for this is that you may find there is a greater purpose behind your articulated higher-level goal in this first iteration of your goal hierarchy. There's a bit more help coming your way that will elucidate this point, before we discuss how this applies to our kids.

2 | Motivation: What Drives You?

Do you want to know what your real motivation is? Then answer this question: what do you do when nobody is watching?

Before we delve into exploring the why behind our goals, let me share with you a personal anecdote and some of the things I picked up whilst assessing hundreds of senior executives for C-suite positions.

Up until my mother's death, my motivations had all been externally driven. I wanted to graduate high school Magna Cum Laude. Then I upped the stakes by wanting to get into an Ivy League University and graduate Summa Cum Laude. Then, after getting my MSc, I wanted to get a job at a top tier investment bank or blue chip consultancy. These external milestones were my personal markers of success: goals created from externally imposed ideals of success. If you make it through the most competitive selection funnels, you must be smart and good and successful, right?

When my mother died, those markers dissipated. Besides realigning my life goals, I began to wonder what was driving me. If these external accolades meant nothing, then what was my driver? As I reflected on my mother's last months, I concluded that you don't take accolades to the grave. The bits you're thinking about on your death bed are the lives you touched, the people you love, the things you wish you had experienced, and the things you want to ensure your loved ones have available to them when you're gone.

After much soul searching and self-analysis, I was able to identify that my biggest driver, the reason why I did what I did, was to help others. I had been motivated to achieve these external drivers because I thought it would make my parents happy because they would be proud of me. In spite of what I now know were their best efforts to help me 'succeed', I hadn't quite realised that it was my *happiness* above all that made them happy. With the beauty of hindsight came the realisation that I was able to achieve those arbitrarily set, externally imposed goals because I actually loved learning. I loved learning for the sake of it, and loved sharing my insights with people around me. This was the beginning of a powerful shift from a world of extrinsic motivation to a world of intrinsic motivation, where the drive became to learn and share what I knew, making an impact, in my own way.

Although it helps to put things into perspective, you need not go through a traumatic experience to make that shift. You just need to be willing to put in some work to understand the difference in motivation types, ask yourself the difficult questions, and be brave enough to engage with the truth.

Intrinsic motivation, or the emotional drive that predicts patterns of behaviour over time, is not made up of choices, values, or a belief system. It is not conscious; if you ask someone what their motive is, they will typically tell you what they value. Intrinsic motivation is about emotions – what people like, enjoy, get energised or engaged by. Intrinsic motivation is also what a person daydreams about and why they pursue the things love, even if they don't have time for them.[8]

The stages of maturity of a motive are about the ability to *channel*, *restrain*, *postpone*, or otherwise *manage* emotional drives – using your desires wisely instead of impulsively. This is exemplified by the 'marshmallow test', the famous exercise to see if a child can wait a little longer to double their marshmallow dosage, or if they succumb to the immediacy of just one when

---

[8] Ryan, 2000.

the researcher leaves the room. Longitudinal studies have confirmed that those who are able to wait for the higher reward go further in life, given the self-regulatory skills they exhibit at an early age. Developing an ability to channel and restrain our motives is highly regarded in business as a way to more effectively reach a top executive position.

Motivation comes in three forms:

- **Extrinsic**: This is a motivation that comes from outside. This can manifest in our attempt to own that big house, or make millions of dollars because we think it sends signals to other people. The internal dialogue will go something like: 'I have to do this.'

- **Intrinsic**: This is a motivation that comes from within. It is intrinsically linked to our personality and preferences. This may entail wanting to help people feel better because it makes you feel better, and may translate into you becoming a doctor because you love the idea of healing people. Thus the internal dialogue may sound something like: 'I like to do this.'

- **Self-Attributed**: This motivation stems from conscious values, which may have been outwardly imposed or internally determined. You may want to be a lawyer because you were told as a young child that seeking justice is the right thing to do. The internal dialogue goes something like: 'It is important that I do this.'

In executive assessment, we try to identify which motivations are intrinsic and self-attributed, because these typically drive a person's behaviours and actions more consistently than extrinsic motivation. After all, what others value may change often, but what we do may have a higher likelihood of staying steady.

It is therefore essential that you spend time identifying your motives (particularly the intrinsic ones), so that you can make sure you're drafting the crispest, clearest goals possible, to sustain that energy, drive, and determination that will enable you to bounce back when times get tough.

What are some of the most common intrinsic motivations people have? Research has shown that three motives occupy 80-85% of daily thinking time.

- **Achievement Motive**: *'I want to do things better, through innovation or efficiency.'* These people typically like to track progress and know their level of accomplishment, and they want to be the best, regardless of whether others know or not. They are not particularly focused on people, but instead on the tasks at hand. They also like self-improvement out of personal interest not requirement, and they tackle challenging yet achievable goals head on. They also tend to make long-term career plans, and are driven by delivering results and functional competence.

- **Affiliation Motive**: *'I want to be part of a group. I want to get along with people.'* These people get satisfaction from being liked or by being friendly to others so as to be part of something bigger than themselves. They think about relationships, enjoy being part of a group, protect their family and friendships, and are loyal to people and organisations. They may worry about whether others like them, will typically choose people over a task, and are driven by collaboration and belonging.

- **Power/Influence Motive**: *'I want to have an impact. I want people to respond.'* These people make an effort to influence others. They like directing the flow of information to influence, and they tend to provide unsolicited assistance or help, as they like to have a positive impact. They tend to be highly aware of people and their motives, and see how organisations work. They can be fantastic at maintaining relationships and being friendly for the sake of influence. They are typically driven by influencing, collaborating, building organisational capability, leading teams, leading change, and they excel in customer focus. (There is also a darker side to the power motive, which is personalised power – this can lead to autocratic, controlling tendencies, but for the sake of our discussion we will focus on socialised power as defined above.[9])

There are more than fifty other motives that can apply to people, in particular in the context of work, but here are the most frequent amongst the remaining ones:

- Security motive: 'I want to be safe'
- Independence motive: 'I want no one to control me'

Some of you may be wondering why I didn't include money here, and there is some research out there stipulating this is certainly a legitimate motivation, but I would argue that money is a proxy for something. Money as a sign of achievement, money to have an impact, money to belong to a certain group, money to have financial independence or to feel safe.

The driver behind some of the most effective CEOs is the influence/power motive, meaning they get energy from seeing people respond, and they love to influence those around them.[10]

What does this mean for you?

Firstly, identifying your motive can be liberating. If you find that you have an achievement motive and you've always wanted to be a manager, you may ask yourself if your desire to be a manager is merely to 'reach the milestone', as opposed to leading people effectively through socialised influence, and if that is the case, you may be able to channel your drive in a way that is more energising to you in the long term. This simple example applies to your life goals. Aligning your goals with your motivations and values will create more coherence and simplicity in your life, allowing you to motor through those resilient, consistent habits that will fuel your energy to get to your goals.

Secondly, creating a hierarchy of your goals will hopefully free

---

[9] Spreier, Fontaine and Malloy, 2006.

[10] McClelland and Burnham, 2003.

40

you from worrying about not completing intermediate or lower-level goals. You will be able to keep things in perspective, and give yourself more leeway to approach the ultimate goal as you see fit, without feeling you've let yourself down by not accomplishing an intermediate one.

Thirdly, this razor focus will allow you to celebrate the smaller wins (short-term goals) along the way, providing momentum and energy to continue to push towards the bigger goals.

Finally, and possibly most importantly, the razor focus will also give you confidence to say no to things that do not align, and to accept you can't be all things to all people. Instead, you can be all things to the people you choose, and to the tasks that you choose to prioritise. In this way we can perhaps see a new meaning to Warren Buffett's famous quote: 'The difference between successful people and really successful people is that really successful people say no to almost everything.' In summary, aligning your goals to your intrinsic motives will help you align your life.

3 | Providing Tools that Enable Self-Discovery, Goal-Setting, and Alignment

Once you're clear on your own goals, and what truly motivates you, you'll also be clearer on your goals for your child. Without that clarity you may send mixed signals to your child, and that can condition their attitude towards success and life overall. Will your objective as a parent be to raise the happiest adult around or will it be to raise the most successful adult around? If you choose the latter, you'll be able to recognise that whatever success means to you will affect your parenting style and lifestyle choices. Hopefully, this book will show you that happiness, well-being, and success are not incompatible, particularly if you choose to redefine success as becoming the most successful version of yourself: to flourish and thrive.

Regardless of your overall objectives, the process should help you recognise that your short-term or intermediate goals for your child may not be your child's goals. (In some instances, your higher-level goals may not be the same as theirs either.) Unless your goals are the same, your child is unlikely to develop the persistence and authenticity of motive required to sustain high performance in spite of adversity. In this case, you can shift your focus away from defining goals for them, and instead focus more on how you can teach them the skills to identify, set, plan, work towards, and celebrate their own goals. It is my hope also, that this exercise will help the tiger parents among us rationally visualise why, if your son/daughter doesn't get into your desired top school (intermediate-level goal) he/she isn't going to be unhappy, unsuccessful or not 'set up for life' (higher-level goal).

So how can you help your child develop the skills to identify their motivation, set goals, and understand their importance besides mirroring that behaviour yourself? As the child matures you may want to share what is in this book with them, but if they are younger, this simple hack from Dr Martin Seligman, featured in his book *The Optimistic Child*, may just do the trick (although there are plenty of other problem resolution and goal-setting techniques that may suit your parenting style better). The next time your child has a problem, use it as an opportunity to start teaching and practising these skills. Instead of jumping in to solve the problem, help them engage higher-level thinking skills, using the following mechanism:

Individually

1) Identify the goal

2) Identify multiple possible pathways to achieving the goal

3) Answer the question 'What can stop you from accomplishing your goal?'

4) Answer the question 'How might you navigate around these obstacles?'

As a Family

5) Share goals and pathways with your family, and brainstorm strategies to overcome obstacles (this may involve alternative pathways to achieve your goal).

Let's work through an example together. Let's say your eldest child smacks his younger sibling (not that difficult to imagine, right?). Once you've ensured the younger child is safe and the older child is calm, pull the older child aside and have a conversation to problem-solve and troubleshoot. The conversation may go something like this (the exact scripting and complexity of language will vary depending on their age):

Parent: *What were you trying to achieve by hitting your sister? (Step 1: Identify the goal.)*
Child: *I wanted my toy and she wouldn't give it back.*
Parent: *I see. It can be frustrating not to get what you want. I bet you felt really angry, maybe even felt a little ball of anger inside, as you thought about how unfair it was that someone took your property* (normalise the emotion, name one of possible values at stake), *but do you think hitting her helped you get your toy back? Has this trick worked for you in the past?*
Child: *Umm … no.*
Parent: *I have an idea. Why don't we come up with better alternatives to get your toy back next time?* (Step 2: Identify alternative pathways to the goal.)

<u>Parent and Child</u>: Proceed to create a list of ideas together. All are valid, even the wildest ones, just write them down on a sheet of paper. Make this feel like a fun brainstorm session, whenever possible.

Parent: *Now that we've got the list, let's see what the advantages and disadvantages of some of these approaches may be.*

<u>Parent and Child</u>: Create a pros and cons analysis of each approach. Cross off the ones that don't work; circle the one that may work best.

Parent: *Now that we've chosen the best strategy, which is asking for the toy back politely with our nicest voice, after paying our sister a compliment first, what do you think can stop you from accomplishing the goal?* (Step 3.)
Child: *Umm … Maybe she still won't give it back.*

Parent: *Yes, that's right. How could we navigate around that?* (Step 4.)
<u>Parent and Child</u>: Create a list of all possible obstacles you can think of, and identify ways to navigate around those obstacles together.

Once you've guided your younger child through this, as they, o older you'd expect them to do Steps 1-4 themselves but then hopefully come to you for Step 5 to brainstorm some other solutions if theirs didn't work. A great way to build a habit around this for a child is to create family infrastructure that supports the task of solving problems creatively together. For example, the simple exercise of asking your kids at dinner about one thing that went well that day, and one thing that didn't go so well can provide plenty of information about any problems they may have experienced or may be experiencing. You can then turn the family dinner table into a team solution-finding session to give the kids plenty of practice. (Imagine what an amazing leader they'd be one day, helping their team learn mastery of this problem-solving skill!)

By doing this, you're setting the neural pathways for your child to think critically about solving problems, whilst realising there are many ways to reach a goal and becoming more flexible in their approach. By acknowledging the things they like, you'll build a mental list that may provide substantial clues to their internal motivations when their personalities are more developed. Later introducing them to the concept of goal hierarchies, you will teach them that it is essential to know what truly motivates them, what they love to do, and what they're good at, in order to set healthy, compatible goals, aligned with a happy, sustainable life.

Recap: Aligning life

✓ Sustainable high performance is achieved by finding persistence and coherence of motive.

✓ Intrinsic (versus extrinsic) motivation is the motivation that energises you to do things because you love to do them. Thus finding your intrinsic motivation will make it more likely that you will stick to your long-term goals.

✓ Define what success looks like to you and confirm it is linked to your intrinsic motivation.

✓ Simplify life success into two to three big *end* goals, and make sure they work *with* each other rather than *against* one another.

✓ Recognise that some goals are *ends* and some goals are *means*, and that means goals can change with time. Abandoning means goals does not signal failure: it signals recalibration and being resilient in your goal pursuit.

✓ Do not be afraid to say no to things that are peripheral to your main goals. It does not mean you are failing; it means you are focusing on the things that truly matter to you.

✓ You may go as far as to build your own goal hierarchy (Exercise II), to crystallise the above and hold yourself accountable, as well as gently remind yourself of what matters when things get a bit more difficult.

✓ Once you have defined success for yourself, become aware of how you are defining success for your child and what markers of success you may be subconsciously or consciously projecting onto your child.

✓ Start paying attention to what drives your child, by seeing what activities they like to engage in and what they seem to value (this will emerge with time).

✓ Help your child develop higher-level thinking and goal-setting skills by engaging them in problem resolution rather than solving problems for them.

✓ When solving a problem, help them identify their objectives, come up with different pathways to reach their goal, analyse the pros and cons of each, think through their preferred course of action, and allow them to try and fail as many times as needed to reach that goal. Serve as a sounding board rather than solving the problem for them directly, to help them build self-efficacy.

✓ Make sure your child understands from an early age that there are many ways to reach a goal, and that the big goals in life should be connected with what they value and love most. This way they won't feel like a failure if they abandon a means (short-term or intermediate-level) goal, and will have a higher likelihood of achieving persistence and coherence of motive, which is key to top performers' success.

Section II

Aligning Mindsets

How do you see yourself?
How do you see others?
How do you see the world?

The answer to these questions can affect your body and your mind. For example:

Did you know that wine tastes better when you believe it is more expensive?[11]

Or that a milkshake can make you fuller if you believe it is more calorific?[12]

That the physical impact of exercise can increase when you are made aware of its benefits?[13]

That your perception of stress can have a huge impact on your health and how you perform under its influence?[14]

---

[11] Plassmann et al., 2008.

[12] Crum et al., 2011.

[13] Crum and Langer, 2007.

[14] Jamieson et al., 2010.

That how fast you learn can depend on your views on intelligence?[15]

As you can see, your mindset can make an impact, but what is a mindset? It is a lens or frame of mind, which orients an individual to a particular set of associations and expectations. In other words, our mindset is the lens through which we see the world, others, and ourselves. Creating an agile, resilient mindset that aligns to the reality of the situation at hand is a crucial component of building resilience.

It logically follows, then, that if we can control our mindset, we can influence a heck of a lot. Scientists are now finding more evidence of how, as per the above list, but philosophers like Aristotle, who coined the concept of 'eudaimonia', were already onto something. This Greek word is commonly translated as happiness or human flourishing.

Whilst Aristotle and the Stoics differed somewhat in their definition and the pre-requisites for eudaimonia, both believed virtue is at the heart of it. Aristotle believed virtue is the most important constituent in eudaimonia, while acknowledging the importance of external goods such as good health, wealth, and beauty. The Stoics believed virtue is sufficient for eudaimonia and did not believe there is a need for external goods. Epictetus, a former slave turned philosopher, and Marcus Aurelius, a former Roman Emperor, both well-known Stoics, wrote philosophical works articulating the fact that one can only control two things: one's actions and one's thoughts, and that doing so was true mastery of oneself, and would lead to happiness and well-being. Today scientists have built upon this work, documenting ways in which eudaimonia also impacts our *performance*.

This section will introduce two mindsets and some 'NeuroHacks', postulated by psychologists and neuroscientists, that will make our brain more agile. This will help us apply the tools outlined in Sections III and IV, enabling us to become the best version of ourselves, and then pass the insight down to our children.

---

[15] Blackwell, Trzesniewski, and Dweck, 2007.

4 | Developing a Growth Versus a Fixed Mindset

It is rare to come across resilience training today that does not include the concept of growth mindset in its midst. Carol Dweck popularised it with her book *Mindset: Changing the Way You Think to Fulfill Your Potential*, and a number of leading schools have already incorporated her teachings into their curriculum with much success.

On a scale of one (strongly agree) to ten (strongly disagree), to what degree you do you agree with the following statement:

Your intelligence is something you can't change

If your answer is closer to one, then you have more of a fixed mindset, and you believe intelligence is a fixed trait. If your answer is closer to ten, then you have more of a growth mindset.

Growth mindset individuals believe intelligence is a malleable quality, a potential that can be developed. They understand that our brain is plastic – it can learn and grow through the process of learning until the day we die.

Neuroscientists explain the biology behind it, for which I will reserve a special place later in the chapter, but its essence means that we make more neural connections, which translates into more creative and clear thinking.

In fact, research shows that telling people to have a growth mindset can backfire. Instead, explaining that *the brain can get stronger and smarter as it learns* has been demonstrated to be most effective.

In the same vein, reiterating the message 'try harder' can also be problematic. The reason is that a growth mindset is more than trying harder. People need to understand *why* they should put in effort and *how* to deploy that effort. Explaining the why behind a growth mindset will also help children develop the skill to ask why more often themselves (and ironically, when they're older, this can help them unearth their intrinsic motivations to 'align life' faster).

So why does having a growth mindset matter? People with a growth mindset outperform those with a fixed mindset, they learn faster, are more open to failure (and merely see it as a way to learn), are more willing to give things a go, and experience lower levels of anxiety. More importantly, growth mindset individuals are more likely to possess intrinsic motivation. As we discussed before, this is the type of motivation that drives you to do better because you enjoy the journey, or because you personally value the outcome, not because of externally imposed values or milestones, giving you more control over what success looks like, and how accomplished you can feel each day, week, month, year. Growth mindset people are more likely to develop goals that resemble something like 'being the best version of myself at X' as opposed to 'beating everyone at X'. The former doesn't focus on competing against anyone else, or depend on obtaining an external accolade. It merely entails putting in the effort, and enjoying the gratification of getting better each day. What a gift! Imagine what it would feel like if upon your attempt to go from 'Couch to 5K' (a training program to get people who have not been exercising much – or don't exercise at all – to start running their first five kilometres), your internal script went something like this:

Day 1: Well done for getting off the couch.

Day 2: Well done for running to the end of the block.

Day 3: Well done for running to the end of the block and two more blocks.

... And so on, instead of the following, which is how I used to speak to myself:

Day 1: This is so hard, I can't even run to the end of the block. All I did was get off the couch. How am I ever going to run 5K like those other people?

Day 2: I'm terrible! I can only run to the end of the block. Look at all those fit people that fit into the tight running clothes and can run around the entire park.

Day 3: Crap, this sucks. I am still tired and I only made it to the end of the block and just a little bit more. I'll never beat James at this rate.

The first person praises themselves, recognising the progress they've made from day to day, not measuring themselves against the 5K objective day in, day out. They will still think about the overall goal of 5K, but they will have broken this down into other smaller goals, and because their objective is to improve their current fitness by showing themselves they can start with a 5K run (rather than run 5K for bragging rights or to beat their friend), they have a mechanism to shower themselves with praise every day, and so they try harder than the previous day. This momentum accumulates and possibly fires bigger improvement leaps.

The second person focuses on what is hard, puts themselves down by comparing their current abilities with others that have been doing this for much longer and have more practice. The second person is also focused on the bigger goal rather than the goal chunking, as there is little to praise until you reach the 5K, if that is your only objective. Guess who will tire themselves out before they've even given the goal a proper shot? Guess who will quit first?

This is why growth mindset people outperform those without. They are more focused on their progress towards the goal than the outcome itself. They have a higher chance of aligning their intrinsic motivations with the externally imposed goals they have chosen for themselves, and they will tend to be 'kinder' to themselves by accepting that challenges, setbacks, and things being difficult are just ways they are moulding their brain into the shape they need to achieve their goal. In the case of the runners, they are creating the neural connections to run more effectively, process oxygen better, increase pulmonary capacity, etc. That in itself will prove motivation enough for those individuals to go and run yet another day, even if they can only make it to the end of the block and back for the first week.

How does this apply to your parenting and your child?

Growth mindset parents can improve their children's performance by helping them embrace this new mindset of being the best version of themselves, and not anyone else's vision of what they should be. They can also help them improve performance while taking the stigma out of failure and reframing that as a way to learn, and make us more capable next time. It also gives parents a wider range of opportunities to praise their child. Rather than praise the child the moment they bring home an A-grade report (which may happen just three times a year in the UK system, or twice a year in most other educational systems), parents would be able to highlight values such as effort, kindness, focus, concentration, and many other qualities that will eventually enhance the likelihood of achieving an A, but that can be observed more frequently. Doing this will not only boost the child's confidence, but it will reinforce the behaviours that are required to 'succeed' in the end. As they will have reframed the ultimate goal into something that is achievable through hard work, this will also give the child more control over outcomes. After all, one cannot control what happens in the end, but one can control how hard one works.

Let's say you buy into all of this, or you already have a growth mindset. You may find that if you were raised in a fixed mindset household or educational system (and many tend to be fixed mindset focused still, given the nature of grades, awards, etc.), there are still some leftovers of this in your mindset and they may manifest without you noticing. So there are a few things we can all do to enhance our growth mindset, whether we believe we are good at it or not (yet).

- **Identify your fixed mindset situations**. It may be that we believe we are good at maths, or we are good at art, or we can't cook, we aren't persuasive, or we are natural salesmen/women, etc. This is a mental construct, a simple manifestation of pre-established beliefs that we hold, or labels we have attributed to ourselves. These beliefs can seep into conversations with our children and accidentally foster a fixed mindset in them. After all, it would be perfectly acceptable for them to mimic your sentence construction and label themselves as good at X, awesome at Y, if they hear you say it about yourself. And labelling is exactly what we want to avoid with a growth mindset. Labelling can be restrictive. Positive labelling runs the risk of our children being worried about losing the label (e.g. being scared to ask a 'silly question' in case they are no longer considered 'clever'). This can be observed in some executive leaders that have come up through some of the most selective funnelling on the planet. These individuals were often told they were clever as kids, yet as adults, roughly 70% suffer from imposter syndrome and many suffer from the 'insecure overachiever complex', the worry that nothing one does is ever enough to prove that you're clever enough, so you need to keep upping the ante to the point of exhaustion or self-annihilation. All this could start with that simple 'you are clever comment' at a young age. (Remember my story about upping the ante with goals from magna cum laude in high school to summa cum laude in college? This is just one of those mindsets I had to proactively change, having been told repeatedly as a child that I was the 'clever' one in the family.) Negative labelling can corner children into a stereotype for the rest of their lives. Have you ever heard a parent tell their child they are naughty? Or ever told yourself 'I am so stupid'? Labelling at a young age can lead to labelling well into adulthood (our parents'/caretakers' external script can turn into our internal script), and turning that inner voice into an inner critic. As Martina Navratilova once said in a different context, 'Labels are for filing. Labels are for clothing. Labels are not for people.'

- **Praise the process**. So what should you do when you want to praise or make a remark to help your child or correct actions? Make sure your commentary focuses on the process, the actions, behaviours, or decisions, but not on the person's character. In other words, instead of 'you are naughty,' use 'you are behaving naughtily' (negative but focused on the action). Or, instead of 'you are clever,' try 'I can tell you focused hard on that exam, as you got a great mark reflecting that' (positive and focused on the actions taken). The latter will remind your child of what they do well, but it will also reinforce the good behaviours that ultimately lead to better outcomes, without putting undue pressure on the outcomes.

- **Watch your language**. Here are a few examples inspired by Carol Dweck's work about how one might correct our language and our child's:

Fixed Mindset	Growth Mindset
I'm not good at this	What am I missing?
I'm awesome at this	What can I improve?
It's good enough	Is it really my best work?
This is so hard, I quit	This is hard, my brain is growing
I can't do this	I can't do this yet
I'm a natural	I worked really hard/practiced a lot
Plan A didn't work	There are more letters in the alphabet

- **Consider ways to be less defensive about mistakes**. By embracing your own mistakes in front of your child, you will not only show them that it's healthy and normal to make mistakes, but you will also create a space for self-acceptance as well as an appreciation that mistakes are part of life and learning. When was the last time you shared one of your mistakes with your child?

Exercise III: Turning a Fixed Mindset into a Growth Mindset

Take a minute to write down your fixed mindset situations. Then write down how else you might explain that situation to yourself.

My Fixed Mindset Situations	Growth Mindset Approach

Once you have done this for yourself, pay attention to your child's fixed mindset situations and write down how you might gently adjust their language to start tweaking their mindset.

Growth Mindset Tips

- Praise Process
- Watch your language
- Identify your fixed mindset situations
- Consider ways to be less defensive about mistakes

5 | Developing a Stress-is-Enhancing Mindset

On a scale of one (strongly agree) to ten (strongly disagree), to what degree you do you agree with the following statement:

Stress is bad for my performance, well-being, and health

If your answer is closer to one, then you have a stress-is-debilitating mindset. If your answer is closer to ten, you have a stress-is-enhancing mindset.

Now this litmus test is not referring to chronic stress. Impacts of the latter type of stress on the brain and our health have been well documented, making it clear that sustained chronic stress is not good for us. But Stanford Professor Kelly McGonigal's recent work, *The Upside of Stress*, explains all the advantages of possessing a stress-is-enhancing mindset. Situational stress can be a gift if only we know how to harness it to power our own performance.

Psychologists have identified three typical reactions to stress:

- **The fight/flight/freeze response**: this occurs when we are highly aroused during a stressful situation and it makes us want to escape, or become overly aggressive, or simply freeze. With this response, our bodies segregate high levels of cortisol (also known as 'the stress hormone'). Cortisol levels may be too high for us to think constructively.

- **The tend and befriend response**: this is when, under stress, we seek to connect, befriend, speak to, or otherwise interact with others. This approach releases oxytocin (a neurotransmitter in the brain also called 'the love hormone'). Here the cortisol is offset by the segregation of oxytocin, and it can help us focus more if need be.

- **The challenge response**: this is when under stress we feel ready and up for the challenge, and have the right level of hormones – high cortisol *and* high DHEA (dehydroepiandrosterone), another hormone that helps us raise our game when it matters. In a wide variety of contexts (academic, business negotiations, sports, military), the challenge response has been shown to drive higher performance than the fight/flight response. And the good news is that we can increase our ability to have a challenge response by developing a nuanced view of stress.

Sometimes we can feel masterful at keeping things in proportion and helping our own stress dissipate, but sometimes, in spite of using all our available tools, *we are still stressed*. In her book, McGonigal, masterfully explains why we face stress even when we are highly effective at keeping things in proportion:

'Stress is what arises when something you care about is at stake'

Within certain limits, stress can be a sign that we are spending time focusing on things that matter to us. In other words, if we are living meaningful lives, some stress may be inevitable.

Thus embracing stress and the positive things it can do for our psychology, physiology, and performance in a given moment, can be an excellent source of our competitive advantage and that of our child.

Scientific studies in public speaking have shown that people who acknowledged they were stressed, that stress can trigger a challenge response, and that a challenge response can enhance performance, were judged to deliver better speeches than those who did not have this nuanced view of stress. Importantly, these high-performing folks were found to be *more stressed* than other speakers, but because they recruited the energy that the stress gave them, they were better at persuading others when they spoke. In other studies, being told 'you're the kind of person whose performance improves under pressure' has itself been shown to improve performance by over a third in certain circumstances.

As well as influencing our unconscious physiological response to stressful situations (i.e. the cortisol to DHEA balance in our system), taking a constructive view of stress can also enhance our conscious coping strategies. When we acknowledge, and even embrace, stress, we are more likely to come up with a plan to overcome or reframe a challenging situation, view it as a growth opportunity, and seek information, help, or advice from others.

So what can one do to start crafting this constructive 'stress-is-enhancing' mindset in challenging situations? McGonigal (2015) recommends three steps:[16]

- **Step 1: Acknowledge stress when you experience it**. Allow yourself to notice it, including its effects on your body.

- **Step 2: Welcome the stress as an adaptive response to something you care about**. Then try to connect to the positive motivation behind your stress. What that you value is at stake and why is it important to you? By tapping into the underlying value at stake, you increase your chances of delivering the challenge response.

---

[16] What follows in this 'stress-is-enhancing mindset' section are excerpts from a Perez Fitzgerald primer, inspired by Kelly McGonigal's work.

- **Step 3: Use the energy that the stress gives you**. Now that you've reminded yourself why the situation is an opportunity for you to express yourself, rather than focusing on 'managing' your stress, take action that reflects your goals and values.

You certainly don't need to view stress as universally positive or meaningful. Often it is unnecessary and unhelpful, such as late at night, when it's more helpful to soothe yourself by focusing on things you appreciate about your loved ones and your life. But by having a more balanced view of stress, you increase your ability to embrace the situations when they arise and use stress as a resource for acting on your goals and values.

Even when you feel like your initial response is more fight/flight, focusing on how you want to respond can shift your biology to support you. One way to increase the chances of this happening is to develop a 'narrative of personal adequacy'. This involves reflecting on all you have achieved in previous stressful circumstances, and reminding yourself in the moment, 'This is good – this is my body trying to help me perform,' or, 'I feel anxious now. That's because I care about this outcome, and I am determined to make it work.'

McGonigal describes embracing stress as a 'radical act of self-trust'. By embracing stress, you are viewing yourself as capable and tapping in to your physical and mental resources. You no longer have to wait for an absence of stress to perform the way you want and be the person you want to be. You give yourself permission to do your best and act on your goals and values when it matters.

How does this apply to your child?

We all know how stressful the UK educational system can be on children. The rise of tiger and helicopter parenting is driving the demands on our children and in turn, the educational system, to levels of unprecedented stress for our little ones. The mere structure of the UK system requiring children to sit exams at the ages of seven, eight, eleven, thirteen, sixteen, and eighteen, brings a series of event-driven stress situations. These higher levels of rising stress are true for children across many geographies, not just the UK. While I am not stating this is a good thing, harnessing the knowledge of situational stress and its impact on performance, if managed wisely and positively, can be a source of strength and confidence for your child, and one they will be able to draw on later into adulthood.

Teaching your child that 'stress is the body's way to get ready for something that is important to you', and that 'stress can give us energy to help us focus and not give up' will go a long way in helping your child cope with those moments. Surviving those moments and changing the way they feel about them will also give them confidence that stress, in the right dosage, is something they can manage, overcome, and use to their advantage. More importantly, embracing a stress-is-enhancing mindset will help your children strike the right balance of stress hormones, which will enhance concentration and focus, and ultimately be better for their health than a less nuanced view of stress that can send cortisol levels through the roof.

Helping your child name the value at stake when they are feeling stressed – e.g. 'I care about doing well in this exam because I like to try my best' or 'I care a lot about doing well in this exam because I want to make Daddy proud' – will give you an insight into the mindset of your child, and thus give you an insight on how to help develop their resilience. If the value at stake is 'I like to try my best', you may have a budding perfectionist on your hands, and may want to highlight how making mistakes and not always getting things right is a learning tool in itself. If the answer is 'I want to make Daddy proud', you may want to reiterate to your child that you are proud of their efforts already and the exam result is not a reflection of that or ever going to change the fact that they worked super hard leading up to it. You will have reinforced the behaviours for success, yet also diffused the tension away from results, and taken the focus away from extrinsic (praise from Daddy) to intrinsic (feeling proud because they worked hard) motivation.

Helping your child identify the value at stake will also get them into the habit of identifying this when they are older, which will subsequently help them identify what actions they need to take to solve the problem at hand. It will turn your child into an 'action-driven solutions finder' rather than someone who ruminates on stress.

Of course, this doesn't just apply to exam-driven stress, although that is one of the most salient sources of stress for children in the school system. These techniques apply to anything your child may deem stressful. I should also highlight that teaching your child when it is appropriate to self-soothe and walk away from a stressful situation is an equally helpful skill.

Exercise IV: Identifying and Harnessing Stress Triggers

For two weeks, keep a journal of what is causing you stress. Try to identify the actual trigger (this could be a sound, smell, a statement, a word, a person, a type of event). Then ask yourself, what value is at stake here? Finally, think about how you can use that energy to take action to alleviate the stress. At the end of the two weeks, take a look at the log and see if there are recurring situations that cause you stress. Then ask yourself if there is anything you can shift structurally to reduce that stress trigger or resolve that situation for good. Your diary may look something like this:

My Stressful Situation	My Stress Trigger(s)	What Value is at Stake?	What Action can I take?
This morning getting the kids ready for school was stressful because we were running late.	When I hear 'Mommyyyyyy ...' in the tone that alerts me they can't find something or don't want to do something.	I care about my children getting to school on time as it teaches them punctuality and respect. I care about getting to work on time for the same reasons. It is important for me to be reliable and to teach my children the same.	Set the alarm clock a little bit earlier. Think about ways to get things done the night before. Delegate more activities to the children.

Once you have done this for yourself, observe what stresses your child. Try to identify triggers, and ask questions. You need not use the word 'stress' and may opt for words like 'worry', 'concern', or 'doubt' if you prefer.

Try sentences like, 'I can see from your expression that you may be worried about something?' or, 'Tell me a bit about what you are feeling?' (If you are particularly interested in effective ways to communicate with your child, I highly recommend

Adele Faber and Elaine Mazlish's book, *How to Talk So Kids Will Listen and Listen So Kids Will Talk*). If you identify a specific recurring trigger, think how you may be able to remove those from the family routine. For example, if your child gets stressed when you are rushing them out the door every morning because they haven't put their uniform on, consider waking everyone up earlier each day and asking the kids to change into uniform before they go down to breakfast. This is a simple example, but it illustrates changing a family routine to solve a typical child stress trigger – running out of time or feeing rushed.

Stress Mindset Tips

- Step 1: Acknowledge stress when you experience it.

- Step 2: Welcome the stress as an adaptive response to something you care about.

- Step 3: Use the energy created by stress – take action that reflects your goals and values.

6 | Leveraging NeuroHacks to Develop Agility

The brain is made up of nerve cells, called neurons, in a network of many connections. Neurons communicate with each other through these connections. The branching parts, called dendrites, receive messages, and the long part, called the axon, transmits a signal through the neuron. When we repeat an action, we use the same neural pathways to send the signal from our brain to our body about what it has to do. The more we repeat that action, the thicker and more easily accessible that part of the brain/action becomes, and the more we go into 'auto pilot' as we no longer need to engage all parts of our brain to execute the action. The flipside of this is that when we learn something new, we have to create the pathways for the neurons to communicate with each other so we can learn the new skill, or codify the new piece of information at hand. This is why we can confidently say to our children that when things feel hard to us, our brain is growing – because it is literally building new neural pathways, which requires energy, and can outwardly manifest in frustration.

According to Rick Hanson, a well-known neuroscientist, our brain has three basic needs, which map to each of the brain's development stages. If any of these needs are unmet, it can cause us stress, turning our mindset from responsive and *agile* – where we can use our brain holistically to think and appropriately respond; to be reactive – to a mindset where only the most primal parts of our brain are engaged, thus clouding our judgment. Let's take a look at these needs and the evolution of our brain to better understand this phenomenon.

Reptilian brain (Hypothalamus)	Paleomammalian brain (Amygdala) Limbic system	Neomammalian brain (Cerebral Cortex)
Safety	Satisfaction	Affiliation
Need to feel safe	Need to feel rewarded/ pleasure/successful	Need to belong

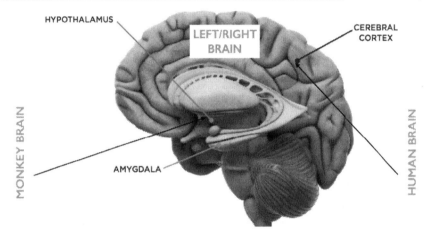

The first stage of our brain's evolution was the reptilian brain. Reptiles were primarily focused on staying safe and out of sight of predators. Thus the first basic brain **need** is to stay alive – or **to stay safe**. Our ancestors were rewarded when they assumed the worst. Those who thought the rustling noise behind the bush was a tiger and ran survived, while others met a different fate. Survival of the fittest ensured we descended from those prone to pessimism and risk aversion. While our environment has drastically changed, our brain's wiring has not evolved as fast, which explains why we can segregate cortisol – the stress hormone – at the sight of a trigger object that reminds us of danger, or in the middle of a performance review when we confuse our manager for a predator!

After the reptilian brain came the paleomammalian brain, also known as the limbic system, where the amygdala resides. This part of the brain **needs satisfaction** – rewards such as pleasure or success. Being rewarded in our limbic system with a hit of dopamine (the reward neurochemical), drove us to find food and water, in spite of difficult circumstances. Today, given the accessibility of food and water, we turn to other items to satisfice this dopamine hit, which in some cases can lead to an addiction to technology, junk food, popularity, cigarettes, alcohol, or drugs. Take our little pleasures away and the dopamine withdrawal sends us into a rage.

Finally came the neomammalian brain, also known as the cerebral cortex, which developed the need for affiliation – **the need to belong**. This drove our ancestors' adherence to the tribe, enhancing their likelihood of survival. Today this manifests in our need to belong to groups, experience what it is like to be in a family, engage in social media where we feel 'connected' to strangers, or work in an office for a strong brand. Feeling shunned or excluded can send us spiralling into withdrawal, feelings of inadequacy, anger, shame, you name it.

If any of these basic neurological needs are unmet – if we feel unsafe, lacking satisfaction/mastery, or like we do not belong – our brain can go into stress mode: what neuroscientists call 'reactive' rather than 'responsive' mode. In its most extreme form, it is also known as an 'amygdala hijack'. To keep the brain agile we need to make sure we are feeling safe, like we belong, and have a sense of mastery.

In more child-friendly terms, the cerebral cortex is described as the 'Upstairs Brain' by Doctors Bryson and Siegel, in their book *The Whole-Brain Child*. The reptilian brain and limbic system are described as the 'Downstairs Brain'. Hold the palm of your hand facing outwards with your thumb next to your fingers, and make a fist. The upstairs brain is the fingertips and the downstairs brain is the palm of the hand. When they are in a fist, the brains are working together; however, when we are stressed, we flip a lid (open your palm entirely), and our upstairs and downstairs brains disengage.

There is an alternative effective description of this phenomenon provided by Professor Peters in his book, *The Chimp Paradox*, where he calls the upstairs brain the 'Human Brain' and the downstairs brain the 'Monkey Brain'. He explains that it almost feels as if we have two brains – the rational, in charge human brain (cerebral cortex), and the brain that feels things intensely, called the monkey brain (reptilian brain and limbic system). Young kids can have fun giving their monkey brain a name (or choosing a new animal altogether) to diffuse a stressful situation, and making animal sounds to represent the fact that their animal brain is in charge.

As we mentioned earlier, when we are stressed, our brain produces the stress hormone, cortisol. This alerts our amygdala and our hypothalamus that something is 'off', and if we act in the moment, our downstairs brain (or monkey brain) is in charge: the amygdala hijack. If we have too much cortisol, we experience bad stress, whereas the right level of cortisol makes our brain agile and enhances our performance.

How does this apply to your child?

There are significant advantages to teaching our kids how to handle stress or an amygdala hijack in the moment beyond making our lives easier during those tantrums, and later full-fledged rows.

Firstly, we can teach our kids about their brains, giving them self-awareness of internal bodily processes that, if left unchecked, can spiral out of their control for years to come. This drives home the point that learning to do this is a process, and it is hard, because we are fighting years of evolution to 'gain control of our brain'. You may want to explain that *'We have two brains – the monkey brain we inherited from animals like reptiles, and the human brain we developed when we became humans.'* (A simplified account, but it works well with little ones.) *'The monkey brain segregates stress juices when it gets upset/mad/angry/stressed/unhappy. Too many of those juices will cloud our judgement and typically make us react in animalistic/instinctive ways (hitting, punching, insulting, shouting, running away, or ignoring the issue). Just enough of those juices allows our human brain to make the good decisions, such as talking about how we feel, finding a solution, and cooperating.'*

Understanding the difference between the two brains can also help soften and diffuse tension in the amygdala hijack moment.

70

Knowing that the monkey brain has taken charge, and calling out their chosen name for it, can sometimes be enough to jolt a child back into engaging the human brain. As you can imagine, overusing this technique could quickly become a way to avoid taking responsibility for the tantrum action (i.e. 'I didn't hit my brother, my monkey brain did!'), so it needs to be used wisely. That said, it can help a child laugh out loud if, in the middle of the tantrum, one can remind them 'Uh-oh, is the monkey in charge now?' taking the onus away from the child to the brain to help them regain composure before analysing their role in the issue.

Secondly, we can explain that what is happening to them is natural and happens to all of us, but that how this manifests is different over time, as we learn to control our brain better as we grow up.

'Finding the right balance of those juices and connecting the two brains when we are upset is hard, I even find it difficult, but we can work on that one step at a time.'

Thirdly, we can explain to them that learning to control our brain can give us a competitive edge by helping us be ourselves more naturally.

'If we learn to do this well, we can stay calm under pressure and make better decisions. This will both maximise the likelihood that you get what you want (although this will not always be possible!), and more importantly, will serve us well later in life.'

Finally, we can give them the tools to better control the brain. This book will present more tools, but there is a simple, fast brain hack that can immediately dissipate stress, if you can manage to engage it. We already said that having a stress-is-enhancing mindset will help, but the single most effective tool to balance out cortisol levels is to **breathe**. This simple act will help the lid flip back down (connecting the animal and human brains once again), and allowing our human brain to help our animal brain think through the situation and ask for help or find solutions. An increased flow of oxygen to the brain will help blood flow and send signals to the body that it is not in danger. This will calm the parasympathetic nervous system right down and send signals to the amygdala that it is safe. When this part of our brain calms down, it gives the human brain a chance to help. If you want to learn more and use illustrated examples to teach your child how this works, Professor Peters has written a fabulous version of *The Chimp Paradox* for children called *My Hidden Chimp*.

Before we close out this mindset alignment section, and while we are here discussing the brain structure, I should bring up Doctor Siegel's research that helping our child integrate the left and right brain is equally as important as upstairs/downstairs, or animal/human. Not only can connecting the two sides promote more of a growth mindset, but it will actually create a bigger corpus callosum – the part of the brain connecting the two hemispheres – allowing our children to make more neural connections, better use of both sides of the brain, and resulting in more agility. The right brain is usually associated with ideas and feelings (arts, music, drama). The left brain is usually associated with logic and structure (maths, engineering).

You may have come across research that stipulates the corpus callosum is wider in women than men, and this is cited as evidence for why women can exhibit a higher degree of emotional intelligence than men (you can choose to agree or disagree with this, as the evidence is mixed!). Some studies are concerned with finding explanations for this discrepancy, and part of this could be attributed to the way we raise little girls and little boys. It is often said to little girls that they use their right brain more than their left brain and vice versa to boys, but how many times have you heard a parent say the following:

Little Girl: *I fell!* (Cries.)
Parent: *Oh my dear, this must hurt. Come here, let me give you a cuddle.* (Comforts her.) *Now, tell me, what happened?*
Little Boy: *I fell!* (Cries.)
Parent: *Get up, be a man. Next time, look in front of you, and be more aware of your surroundings.*

That little girl is going to tap into her right brain by verbalising her emotion and being allowed to cry. Her senses are stimulated when she is cuddled and comforted, further connecting to her right brain and downstairs brain (reward, safety). Then she is going to engage her left side of the brain (and upstairs) to analyse what happened. In contrast, that little boy is just being told to suck it up. He isn't being allowed to explain how he feels, or to cry out the tension. He is offered a rational explanation for something he can do to fix this, appealing to the left brain and upstairs brain, but there has been a missed opportunity to connect various parts of the brain and to stimulate the senses to meet some of the basic brain needs of safety, satisfaction, and even affiliation.

I am by no means postulating that this is the reason why corpus callosum may be different in men than women, nor am I saying that most parents raise their kids this way; I am merely using this as an example of missed opportunities to connect the two sides of the brain, which may or may not be gender specific depending on the lens through which one raises one's child. No matter how you choose to raise yours, allowing children to verbalise how they feel when they are having an amygdala hijack, helping them calm down to engage the upstairs brain through breathing, naming their 'monkey brain' and laughing, and then bringing in a logical explanation for what is happening to them, is just another way to help children create a thicker corpus callosum, which will inevitably lead to enhanced learning agility and emotional intelligence. It will give them better intrapersonal awareness, self-regulation, and a greater ability to relate to empathise and help others – skills largely correlated not only with managerial and leadership success, but arguably also making them nicer human beings.

Now that we have learned ways to enhance our brain's agility by understating its three basic needs, what happens when we experience stress, how we can have a learning attitude, and how our brain's physiology impacts the way we react to adverse events, we are ready to start learning some tools to handle adversity by engaging our cerebral cortex (the upstairs/human brain).

Recap: Aligning Mindsets

✓ Growth mindset individuals understand that our brain is plastic – it can learn and grow until the day we die.

✓ People with a growth mindset outperform those with a fixed mindset, they learn faster, embrace 'failure' as a way to learn, are more willing to give things a go, and experience lower levels of anxiety.

✓ Growth mindset parenting can help your child experience lower levels of anxiety, embrace mistakes as learning, accept themselves, and experience mastery and self-efficacy more often.

✓ Help your child set increasingly challenging goals in relation to things they value and have at least some control over, such as working hard or being the best version of themselves, as opposed to measuring themselves purely against externally imposed mileposts. This will develop intrinsic motivation and self-efficacy.

✓ Help your child understand that their brain is growing when something feels hard, or when they make a mistake, and that this will allow them to reach their goal in the long term.

✓ Separate behaviour/action from character. Use 'you're acting naughtily' as opposed to 'you are naughty', or 'you made a bad decision, but that doesn't make you a bad person.'

✓ Praise the process, behaviour or character traits such as hard work, kindness, thoughtfulness, and curiosity, not outcomes or results such as winning, grades, levels, awards, and titles.

✓ Watch your language: 'I can't do this *yet*.'

✓ Having a stress-is-enhancing mindset can boost performance and well-being.

✓ Remind yourself (and your child) that situational stress can power performance, that nerves are your body's way of getting ready, that there is a value at stake that you care about, and that utilising the energy to work towards your goal will fuel your achievement of it.

✓ The brain has three basic needs – mastery, safety, affiliation – which, if unmet, can trigger an amygdala hijack response.

✓ The brain is composed of an upstairs brain (prefrontal cortex/human brain) where our executive functions and thinking reside, as well as the downstairs brain (limbic system/animal brain), where our primary instincts and strong feelings reside. We make the best decisions when both of these are connected, but they disconnect during an amygdala hijack.

✓ Breathing is a good way to engage the parasympathetic system, helping us regain control of our instinctive reaction during the amygdala hijack.

✓ The brain also has a left brain (usually associated to logic and structure) and right brain (usually associated to ideas and feelings). We make the best decisions when we connect both sides.

✓ When solving a problem, or in a stressful situation, engage the whole brain. Understand when your child is in amygdala hijack mode, help them calm down. Ask them to verbalise their emotion, normalise it, and help them think through a solution to activate those neural connections.

Section III

Building Reactive Resilience

Ever found yourself reacting strongly and negatively to an adverse event, where the emotion seemed out of proportion with the situation? Perhaps your partner misplaces a teacup and you go ballistic on them? Well, you're probably not alone.

Psychologists argue that the way a person explains a bad event is largely correlated with how their **primary caretaker** (parents, guardians, nannies, teachers, coaches, etc.) explained bad events when they happened during their childhood, and that without much intervention, this explanatory style is lifelong. Explanatory styles are the little stories we tell ourselves (and often share with others) to make sense of our life. People can have either optimistic or pessimistic explanatory styles, and the research points to a correlation between positive explanatory style and academic and career success, higher levels of health, and reduced likelihood of depression. So the next time your kid spills the milk, or you lose a sale, or believe you've failed at something, notice – how are you explaining this to yourself? What is the mental script running through your head? And, more importantly, what are you teaching your child when you explain these bad events out loud?

Psychologists now understand that there is an optimal way to explain events to nurture your mental health and overall resilience, and this approach is either natural to you (because you may have learnt it from a strong role model) or you can develop it as of now.

This section will introduce techniques to change the way you explain bad events, and to separate events from feelings, enabling you to take charge of your moods and your actions. Building these skills will help you, and in turn, your children to develop a more balanced and realistic set of emotions, and help us build relationships, in particular self-acceptance, as well as raise awareness of cognitive distortions and begin to problem-solve.

7 | Developing a Healthy Explanatory Style

How you react when your child spills the milk is creating neural pathways in your child's brain, and it could easily affect the way your child explains their inability to get the CEO job (or whatever they set their heart on) to themselves in the future. As we've discussed, optimistic explanatory styles have been linked to higher levels of performance, achievement, and health. In fact, research shows that optimists bounce back from failed exams, divorce, unemployment, and disability, while pessimists give up easily, and are more prone to depression. These differences can be far-reaching, as optimists are more likely to be successful in almost all areas of pursuit, including relationships, business, general health, sport, and academic success.

The good news is that if your natural explanatory style is more pessimistic, you can teach yourself how to change that for the benefit of yourself and your child. The **explanatory styles** of pessimists versus optimists are easily distinguished in three predictable ways, known as the 3Ps:

- **Personalisation (also known as self-attribution):** This dimension is concerned with the perception of causality. Who is at fault? Is it your fault or the outside world? *Events can be internally or externally caused:*

Say you lose a tennis match. A pessimistic player will interpret the cause as personal ('I missed way too many shots. I failed to win.'). This contrasts with an optimist, who allows for non-personal factors ('It wasn't my day today. My opponent had an incredible day; they played better.').

As Seligman[17] points out, you may be interested to know that women tend to personalise much more than men. In fact, research has shown women have a 50% higher likelihood of experiencing depressive symptoms, and a large part is due to this, as well as the fact that women will ruminate more when things go badly, as opposed to shifting focus to another activity. This is not the case in young children, where boys and girls show the same level of optimism, with a slight advantage to girls, until the teenage years, where this balance starts to tip in favour of boys.

- **Permanence:** This dimension relates to the perception of time. Do you believe the bad event is temporary or lasts forever/ happens all the time? *Events are perceived as permanent or temporary:*

Pessimists interpret setbacks as permanent ('I'll never be in the top team'). In contrast, an optimist sees the setback as only temporary ('If I work harder, maybe I'll make it at the next try-outs').

- **Pervasiveness:** This dimension relates to the perception of space. Do you believe the bad event happens in this specific situation or in every aspect of your life? *Events are perceived as global or specific:*

Pessimists see setbacks as all-pervasive ('Nothing ever works out for me'). In contrast, the optimist sees the setback as narrowly contained or confined to one area of life ('I may have done poorly at the try-outs today, but I did well in the match yesterday, and I am a hard worker').

It is also important to highlight that the first P (personalisation) can often be mistaken with blame versus taking responsibility.

---

[17] Seligman, 1998.

When I've conducted workshops and explained to people that an optimist's preferred explanatory style when things go well is to take credit, and that their preferred way to explain bad events is to blame external factors, people ask me if they are meant to become delusional. The answer, of course, is no. The idea here is to identify the part you played in the bad event and acknowledge responsibility for it (and learn from it for the future), but to put that in balance with all the other factors that contributed to that outcome. In the example of the tennis match, one could have concluded: 'I missed a lot of forehands today. That is typically one of my weaker shots and I am working on it. On the other hand, the conditions were tough due to the wind, and my opponent seemed to exploit my forehand. They played well, so although I tried my best, it just wasn't good enough today. I will need to practise my forehand some more'. This will ensure that self-esteem is intact but that responsibility and ownership for what we can do better is also paramount.

In reality, positive psychology acknowledges that, 'optimism can have costs if it is too unrealistic'.[18] Seligman also cautions individuals to avoid optimism if you are trying to plan for a risky or uncertain future.[19] In fact, he goes as far as to state that successful lawyers have a more pessimistic explanatory style. This is because pessimism helps us maintain caution, prudence, and analytic thinking, all key components to the effective decision-making required of the world's top lawyers.

The goal is not to become purely optimistic and eliminate pessimistic thoughts. Instead, it is about choosing the type of explanatory style that will be most effective for a given situation, and remembering that the type we choose has the ability to impact our feelings, moods, and ultimately, our actions.

---

[18] Peterson, 2000.

[19] Seligman, 1990.

With that in mind, let's take a look at a tool that will help us challenge our thinking and will require the selection of the best explanatory style to do so.

8 | Leveraging the ABC Model to Adequately Respond to Adversity

The ABC model[20] is a core resilience skill, allowing the individual to identify why they feel certain ways in different situations. An (A) activating event triggers a (B) belief or thought, and this drives a (C) consequence in our emotions, behaviour, and actions.

Many people assume that the (A) activating event leads directly to the (C) emotional consequence, but what this model allows the individual to do is to identify the underlying (B) belief or thought that is really intermediating between the event and the consequence.

Knowing this can help the individual to understand their reaction to certain situations, and to evaluate whether or not the thought that is driving their reaction is helping or harming them. When their underlying thoughts are counterproductive, they can learn to (D) dispute them so that they feel (E) energised to take action (extending 'ABC' to 'ABCDE').[21]

The ABC tool has been used by The Penn Resilience Program, designed to help the US Army and their families enhance their mental and physical resilience. The tool has also been effectively

---

[20] Reivich and Shatte, 2002.

[21] Seligman, 2002.

rolled out to children across select schools in the United States and the UK with great success. It is an evidence-based tool, which enables higher levels of performance, and it can be learnt. The results speak for themselves in that it has been proven to reduce depressive symptoms by keeping things in perspective. Teaching ourselves and others to not assume and instead seek (dis)confirmation and work from facts to decatastrophise events that feel overwhelming, will not only help us regain control in difficult times, but it will also enhance our performance in the long term.

Let's bring this to life with a personal example of ABC in action.

Growing up all around the world made me conclude that change was *always* something to look forward to – something additive, where one gained new friends and maintained old ones. My dad worked in the oil industry, which is why I lived in over twenty-one cities and four continents by the time I turned twenty-four. The reasons we moved as a family were due to my father's relentless ambition, which was rewarded with promotions and new challenges. His ambitious and growth-orientated mindset (and stated and *unstated* expectations) rubbed off on me, and I grew up always gunning to reach the C-suite.

So when I finally got my chance to join the executive committee of a philanthropy in 2014, I was over the moon. This philanthropy was the second largest in the world, based in over seventy countries. I had joined them to build the talent function from scratch, having never worked in HR nor in the not-for-profit sector before. So it will strike you as no surprise that I spent a lot of time preparing, listening, and observing behaviours to ensure I could fit right in. Yet my first big presentation in my new role was one of the worst days of my professional career.

After a three-month worldwide listening tour, my first task was to build a 360 tool for the eighteen-person strong executive committee. The aim was to get a view on performance, but more importantly to help each of them develop into the best version of themselves through integrated feedback. This was rather novel at the foundation, as some people had worked in this philanthropy for over twenty years and had rarely, if ever, received a performance review before. In fact, there seemed to be a consensus across various pockets of the foundation that delivering feedback would hurt people's feelings, so most shied away from providing it. Considering the senior leadership team historically operated as individuals competing for resources, asking them to become a peer group was a challenge in itself, let alone asking them to provide objective feedback on each other.

I trod carefully in the lead-up up to my first big meeting to finally get the green light to take the 360 project forward. I listened, benchmarked, got ongoing feedback from key people, ran a pilot, and provided a required memo outlining the rationale, context, developmental process that the project would entail. My work met with encouragement. This was my chance to make a big impression, to mark the beginning of our cultural transformation journey, and to get their final seal of approval and buy-in for the process.

When my presentation finally took place, it was an unmitigated disaster. Those who had supported me in the pilot turned against the exercise; those who had read the pre-wire materials but provided no feedback beforehand spoke up grossly against my proposals. I could feel my hands getting clammy, my throat getting patchy, and my muscles tightening. I took deep breaths, smiled, and listened. The building tension left me tongue-tied, and almost unable to respond. I left the meeting feeling embarrassed, demoralised, and betrayed.

So what happened to me there? Before we examine that, remember that examples of adversity don't have to be one-offs such as this monumental meeting: we face adversity every day. An abrupt email from the CEO causes anxiety; being cut across in traffic causes anger; a friend cancelling a holiday at the last minute, or your child getting left out of a party causes you to feel rejected. When these things happen, most people think that events drive our emotions and therefore our response...

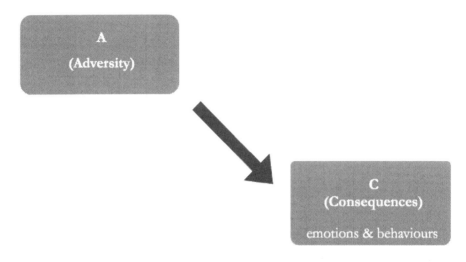

. . .But of course, it's not quite that simple. The biggest drivers of how we react to adversity are the beliefs we hold about the causes and consequences of the adversity we face. If our beliefs are erroneous and/or unhelpful, they can lead to maladaptive behaviours, which look more like this:

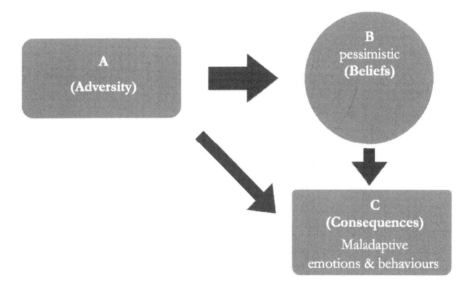

So what happened to me at the presentation? Was my (C) emotional reaction caused by the (A) meeting itself? Was that one meeting really that important? Did the (A) adversity of failing to get the desired response lead me to (C) feel dejected, demoralised, betrayed, anxious, and embarrassed?

No, as we saw before, it was not the situation that led me to feel that way, instead my (B) beliefs about the situation that caused how I felt.

In other words, my mind can control how events make me feel, and in turn, what I do to resolve them.

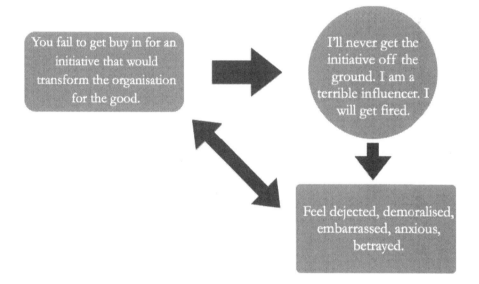

We can control our mindset by interrupting downward spirals, thinking traps, or our own cognitive distortions by learning to dispute destructive beliefs.

How do we do this? We can look for evidence to support or refute our belief, and we can brainstorm alternative explanations for the adversity we face.

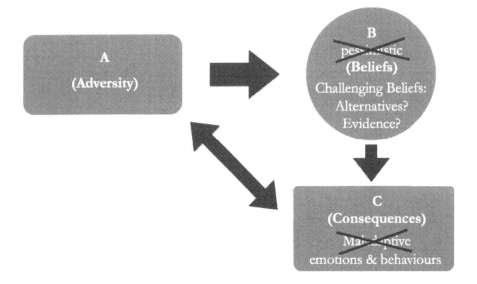

In my case I could've thought:

- Just because I like new things and change, doesn't mean everyone does. Change is typically stressful, maybe this is about their reaction to change and not so much about me or my abilities.

  - Maybe they are insecure about losing their jobs through this exercise, and I am experiencing countertransference as a result, which explains why I was feeling insecure about losing my own.

  - Maybe, rather than betraying me, some felt they couldn't lose face by disagreeing with the rest of their colleagues in public, given the low levels of trust in the group.

- They know I can influence, as they've already noted how I have changed and influenced various things since my arrival; they may think I wasn't at my best this time, which is not permanent and can be changed.

- Maybe the memo and my meetings just weren't enough, maybe they didn't have all the information I thought they had at hand, and maybe a one-hour meeting wasn't enough to cover it all.

- I earned this job and have already made a positive impact; I can take this opportunity to show them just how well I can do it by acting quickly on the new feedback to earn further trust.

So you see, by challenging the beliefs that are driving our emotions (considering alternative interpretations and testing them for accuracy by seeking out more evidence), we can reassume control of our emotions and respond in a constructive way to challenging circumstances. This is called (D) Decatastrophising to (E) Energise (identifying what action can be taken). So the model is truly an ABCDE model shortened to ABC.

So what did I do?

After the presentation, I flew to NYC where the majority of the executive committee was based. I met with each of them 1:1 and listened. I listened to their fears and anxieties, and I tried to appease them by explaining and reiterating once again, *and in person*, that the tool would focus, as did the philosophy of our talent function, on identifying their strengths. That we would help them make their unconscious competence consciously competent so they could teach their strengths to their teams, and that their developmental feedback would be confidential. Their gratitude taught me that at least some of my decatastrophising thoughts were more accurate than my immediate beliefs about the situation. One week later, after tweaking some language reflecting their responses, we launched the tool. One year later, it was the most widely used development tool in the organisation, above coaching, training, mentoring, or any other L&D strands.

Exercise V: Getting Started with ABC

Get a piece of paper and draw two lines, writing A, B, and C at the top of each of the columns created.

It could look something like this:

A	B	C
Activating Event	**Beliefs and Thoughts**	**Consequences**
Can be big or small, good or bad	*What was running through your head in the moment*	*How did you feel and what did you do in response?*

1. The first step is to get in the habit of noting down our A and C column pairs. What is the adversity? Use the five senses to describe it only, sticking to the facts of the situation. What is the consequence? How does it make us feel and act?

2. The next step is to fill in the B column – this is the place you can write down what was going through your head during the adversity. Were you:

- Blaming yourself (personalising) or blaming the outside world (externalising)?

- Assuming this is a character flaw (permanent) or a lapse of judgement (temporary)?

- Assuming this made you bad at other things in your life (pervasiveness) or this is a specific situation?

- If none of the above apply, that's okay. Just write down your script as precisely as you recall it.

It could end up looking like this:

A	B	C
Activating Event *Can be big or small, good or bad*	**Beliefs and Thoughts** *What was running through your head in the moment*	**Consequences** *How did you feel and what did you do in response?*
Someone pulled out in front of me in traffic on my way to work, and I had to break sharply.	*'What a selfish idiot. What makes them think their needs are more important than mine?'*	*I felt hostile and beeped my horn. My heart was pounding and I was anxious that I'd be late for work.*

3. The final step is to keep repeating this exercise for a good two weeks each time you face an adversity, big or small. This will serve as a log for you to keep track of your most frequent thinking traps.

Once we have a good evidence log of what our (A) adversity, (C) consequence, and (B) belief clusters are, we can then get more sophisticated in our negative thought combatting skills. In fact, we can start to see patterns in the way we are thinking – the traps we seem to be falling into – so that we can prevent succumbing to them in the future. As we have discussed, explanatory style encompasses three possible thinking traps (personalisation, permanence, and pervasiveness), also known as cognitive distortions – inaccurate thoughts that undermine our response to given situations.

That said, there are plenty more distortions that we have inherited for good evolutionary reasons that may have now outlived their purpose. In the following exercise, I list the most common ones I witness during our workshops.

Exercise VI: Identifying Cognitive Distortions

This exercise will help you raise awareness of your go-to cognitive distortions.

1. Read through the list of additional cognitive distortions, and notice which ones jump out at you.

2. Go back to the evidence log you created as part of Exercise V, and see if you can spot any patterns that relate to any of the distortions outlined here.

Distortion	What it is
Permanence	Believing a passing negative event will persist over time
Pervasiveness	Believing a negative event in one domain (e.g. work) will pervade other domains (e.g. home)
Personalising	The tendency to *automatically* attribute an event to one's personal characteristics or actions
Externalising	The tendency to *automatically* attribute an event to other people or circumstances
Maximising and Minimising	Errors in evaluating events in which the negative aspects of a situation are magnified and the positive aspects are minimised (or vice versa)
Jumping to conclusions	Believing one is certain of the meaning of the situation despite little or no evidence
Overgeneralising	Settling on global beliefs about one's general lack of worth or ability on the basis of a single situation
Mind-reading	Assuming that you know what the other person is thinking, or expecting the other person to know what you are thinking
Emotional reasoning	Drawing conclusions about the nature of the world based on your emotional state

In the rare event that your log doesn't match any of these examples, pay attention to your reactions to people and situations in the coming week and ask yourself if you may be doing any of these. I have typically found that those who mind-read aren't always conscious that they are doing it. In fact, because these are traps, we are often unaware we fall into them, thus it may take a while until you can start to recognise them in yourself. That said, you may find it easier to recognise these traps in other people including your children, so you may want to consider asking a close friend/spouse/co-worker to see if they can spot any in you.

Once you've had enough time to observe and log your ABC clusters and analyse the cognitive distortions that you may be showing a preference for, you're ready to go for the full ABCDE approach. Some of you may just want to go here from the start, and that is okay too.

Exercise VII: Bringing it All Together – ABCDE

Draw four lines on a piece of paper and label each at the top A, B, C, D, E. It may look something like this:

A	B	C	D	E
Activating Event	**Beliefs and Thoughts**	**Consequences**	**Decatastrophise /Reflection**	**Energise**
Can be big or small, good or bad	*What was running through your head in the moment*	*How did you feel and what did you do in response?*	*How accurate and/ or helpful were your beliefs? How did you (or could you have) checked them? What differences would that have made? ID your cognitive distortion*	*What are the helpful and accurate beliefs that you would rather buy into when this kind of activating event happens again?*

1. Log the (A) activating event – big or small, stick to the facts.

2. Log the (C) consequences – how did you feel, and what did you do in response?

3. Log the (B) beliefs and thoughts – what was running through your head in the moment?

4. Log the (D) reflection and cognitive distortion – how accurate and or helpful is the belief? How did you or could you check them? What difference would a different belief have made? NAME the cognitive distortion.

5. Log the Action (E) – what are the helpful and accurate beliefs that you would rather buy into when this kind of event happens in the future? And what action can you take now to use the nervous energy for good?

Your final ABCDE entry for this particular issue may end up looking like this:

A	B	C	D	E
Activating Event	Beliefs and Thoughts	Consequences	Decatastrophise/ Reflection	Energise
Someone pulled out in front of me in traffic on my way to work, and I had to brake sharply.	What a selfish idiot. What makes them think their needs are more important than mine?'	I felt hostile and beeped my horn. My heart was pounding and I was anxious that I'd be late for work.	Maybe they were being selfish. But perhaps they didn't see me and were under a lot of pressure? When I contemplated this possibility, I calmed down and arrived at work in a better mood. *Cognitive distortion: mind-reading*	If I face a similar situation, then I'd like to avoid reading others' minds – and when I do, I'd like to assume that they have positive intent. I know that when people assume the worst about me they are usually wrong (so my belief is likely be accurate), and I know that when I assume positive intent, I react in a more constructive way (so my belief is likely to be helpful).

If you need more help reflecting on your thinking traps or resolving them, take a look in the chart further down for some tips.

I won't fall into thinking traps but I know what you're thinking (yup, I'm mind- reading now). You're probably thinking this is a lot of work, but that it looks like it could be helpful. You may mark this page and think you'll come back to it later. That is all okay (if that is, in fact, your thinking)! All I'd love to highlight here is that applying ABC is like developing a muscle. It will feel awkward, tedious, and possibly useless at first (although for those of us that are a little scatter-brained, just the mere act of writing things down in an organised fashion can be enough to experience stress relief.) This will change across time. The more you do this exercise, the easier it will become (growth mindset). Once you've identified your top three cognitive distortions and you've written out your D and E columns, they can become your internal mental 'decatastrophising script'. In time, this will be something you do naturally inside your head and halt the negative thoughts that would have otherwise affected you for days, weeks or months, in just a day, a few hours, a minute, and eventually not at all. The brain is a muscle that grows, and this is a new neural pathway you need to create (or widen if you already do some form of this) so as to make it a part of your mental arsenal.

Distortion	What it is	How to overcome it
Permanence	Believing a passing negative event will persist over time	Identify 'three-day impact': in three days' time, how big of a deal will this be?
Pervasiveness	Believing a negative event in one domain (e.g. work) will pervade other domains (e.g. home)	Identify scope of domain: where does this situation fit?
Personalising	The tendency to *automatically* attribute an event to one's personal characteristics or actions	Look outward: what external factors/people played a role?
Externalising	The tendency to *automatically* attribute an event to other people or circumstances	Look inward: How did I contribute to the situation?
Maximising and Minimising	Errors in evaluating events in which the negative aspects of a situation are magnified and the positive aspects are minimised (or vice versa)	Be even-handed: what other aspects (positive or negative) should I consider?
Jumping to conclusions	Believing one is certain of the meaning of the situation despite little or no evidence	Slow down: what else could be going on here?
Overgeneralising	Settling on global beliefs about one's general lack of worth or ability on the basis of a single situation	Look at behaviour: is there a specific behaviour that explains the situation?
Mind-reading	Assuming that you know what the other person is thinking, or expecting the other person to know what you are thinking	Speak up: what could you say or ask to increase understanding?
Emotional reasoning	Drawing conclusions about the nature of the world based on your emotional state	Separate feelings from facts: are my feelings accurately reflecting the facts of the situation?

How does this apply to your child?

Psychologists like Seligman believe that this tool can be taught to children as young as seven, and that you can work up the level of complexity as they start to master the ABC basics. For example, you probably wouldn't introduce cognitive distortions with all their jargon at seven, but you may explain the 3Ps with plain language when helping your child describe a bad event. As they grow older, you may share more cognitive distortions and their solutions as appropriate, and as you observe them in your child, their friends, yourself or someone known to you both, to illustrate it as a living example with consequences.

If they are younger than seven, you can start helping them in a counter-intuitive way. Firstly, do *not* attempt to solve their problem when they bring it to you right away. Often as parents our first reaction when our child has a problem is to either deny the problem exists, minimise it, or just solve it for them. Problems are within the scale of the age and the time, so what can seem like a small problem to you (i.e. 'he won't share the toy with me') may be a huge deal to them. Thus it shouldn't be entirely dismissed; it can serve as an effective watered-down ABC lesson.

The first step is to acknowledge their issue (name the adversity, A), and make them feel heard (outline how they feel, C), to help them reason through it (challenge their B column). The second step is to plant the seeds of seeking evidence for our assumptions or choosing more helpful beliefs (the beginning of column D). For those older children towards the four-to-seven range, depending on your child's ease in social situations, you can then add a socially developed skill section of going out to seek the alternative evidence so they can take action to resolve it (Energise, E)

You are going to verbally help them do the following:

1) Outline the problem (name the **A**dversity)

2) State and legitimise how they feel (name the feeling and action/ **C**onsequence)

3) Share what their thoughts are about it (state their **B**eliefs)

4) Challenge their thinking (plant seeds of Decatastrophising)

5) Empower your child to take action (Energise)

Here is an example:

Child: Jack said he didn't want to be my friend any more.
Parent: Oh. (Empathic glance but doesn't give too much away so as to not condition response.) *How did that make you feel?*
Child: Really angry. I hate Jack.
Parent: I can see you feel angry and hurt; it must be tough to hear that. Tell me what happened? (Listen to their explanation.) Why do you think he said that he didn't want to be friends?
Child: Because he is mean. He always says mean things to me.
Parent: It may feel like that now, but can you remember all the times Jack has said nice things to you before? And all the times he called you his best friend? That doesn't mean he didn't say it this time and that it doesn't hurt your feelings, but can we think of other reasons why Jack may have said what he did?
Child: Mmm…
Parent: (Listen to any alternatives your child comes up with.) Sure, and what about… (You can turn this into a fun guessing game and alternatively provide suggestions as follows:)

- Maybe he was just angry and didn't mean it?

- Maybe someone was mean to him that morning and he was feeling bad about himself and thought being mean to someone else may make him feel better?

- Or perhaps he got in a fight with his parents that morning and was feeling upset?

- Maybe he just woke up in a bad mood?

- Or maybe he didn't like it when you took the toy from him and he didn't know how else to tell you to give it back?

None of these reasons make Jack's reaction right, but it may explain why it happened, and that may make you feel differently about him. Perhaps you feel bad for him instead of being angry with him?

Child: *Yes, maybe.*

Parent: *How do you think you can find out which of these it was?*
Child: *Maybe I can ask him?*
Parent: *Good idea. I've often found the best way to say how I feel without hurting others' feelings is to tell them how their actions made* me *feel and then politely ask if they meant to do that. So, for example, you may want to say the following to him: 'Jack, when you said you didn't want to be my friend, it hurt my feelings. Did you mean that?' I bet you'll find that there was another reason for why he said it. I also got into fights with my friends when I was your age and said things I didn't mean – it's all part of growing up and learning to communicate with one another. Let's see what you find out and we can deal with it then.*

So you see, this tool isn't just about combatting our negative thinking, it can also be a great way to develop social and emotional intelligence by getting to know ourselves better, as well as those around us. Not taking things for granted, mind-reading or jumping to conclusions will empower us to ask more questions, and seek evidence to challenge our thoughts. If we tend to be the type of people that assume the worst in others, questioning more will likely provide us evidence that others are 'not so bad'. If we tend to be the type of person that assumes people blame us for things, asking people if that is the case will probably liberate us from feeling this way. As the Stoics said, we cannot control much, but **we can control our thoughts and our actions**. This tool is a brilliant way to do both of these things more often, and, most importantly, to help us act in proportion with the situations that arise in our lives, giving us the chance to bounce back from adversity faster.

9 | Harnessing Reset Buttons to Turn A Bad Day Around

We have just introduced a rather cerebral way to deal with negative thinking loops. The process we've outlined entails first being aware that we are entering a negative thinking loop, then identifying the source of thoughts that are creating the loop, then identifying the actual thought, analysing the thought, combatting the thought, identifying better or more helpful thoughts to replace that with, and energising in order to take action to alleviate our negative thinking. All that is a lot of thinking! While this exercise is certainly helpful, it is an investment, and may not always work, especially if your child isn't emotionally ready.

Sometimes what we need is a distraction, something to jolt us out of thinking mode and into action mode. It may be that we need to gather a bit of perspective, calm ourselves down, or just make ourselves feel physically better, so that we can then use the ABC (DE) tool appropriately with more time and in a better mental state.

So what do you do to get yourself into a better mental state if you don't want to use ABCDE or the time just isn't right for it? For many of us, the answer is something like 'I feel anxious' or, 'I procrastinate' or, 'I don't feel 100% for the rest of the day'. But it doesn't have to be that way. Identifying personal 'reset buttons' that help you get back on track when your day is not working out as you had planned or hoped is a potent technique.

Reset buttons are things that we deliberately do to renew ourselves emotionally and physically. They can help us overcome procrastination or negative emotion that is building up and prepare for whatever is coming next.

Remember when we talked about NeuroHacks and the importance of breathing to take control away from the downstairs brain towards the upstairs brain? Or when we said naming the downstairs brain with a funny animal name and using that in the middle of the amygdala hijack could be helpful to generate laughter and change the dynamic? We must make ourselves feel better when decatastrophising in order to engage the prefrontal cortex before taking action under stress. Reset buttons are just that – they could include a simple breathing exercise, but they could also include a number of things, and following are some examples that people have often brought up in our workshops:

- Remind myself how far I have come this year
- Read my happy folder (a folder one keeps with nice notes, thank you cards, or meaningful messages one has received to celebrate important milestones)
- Take a nap
- Relive a good moment in the past
- Visualise a nice moment in the future
- Look at pictures
- Go for a run
- Listen to my favourite playlist or build a new one
- Write a thank you note
- Take the dog for a walk
- Call my mum
- Practise some deep breathing

- Watch my favourite comedy
- Take a long shower/bath
- Have a tea/coffee
- Go to the gym
- Watch an inspirational film
- Play tennis with friends
- Watch thirty minutes of fun videos on YouTube
- Go to yoga

Exercise VIII: Reset Buttons

Take a moment to reflect on what you do to renew yourself physically or emotionally. What is your first instinct when you're feeling down? What types of activities help you feel better?

Self-Reflection: What are my reset buttons?

Self-Reflection: What are my child's reset buttons?

After taking a stab at answering on behalf of your child, you may want to observe or ask them, what types of activities they naturally turn to when they can choose what to do. Knowing this is a powerful way to turn a bad day around without having to wait to get out of the funk. It can empower you to take charge of your mood and your day. Imagine helping your child identify theirs: it will help them internalise that they have it within themselves to feel better.

Whilst ABC will help them to tame their thoughts, reset buttons will teach them that little things can go a long way to change one's mood. Identifying this will also help them get more in touch with their feelings, emotions, and the things that they love. This will allow them to find strength and drive and sustained persistence of motive, because it will invite them to look within themselves and find out what they like, and how this impacts their levels of energy and ultimately, drive. Instead of looking to adults to guide them to activities they may or should enjoy, they will start being more aware of the physical clues our bodies give us that guide us towards happiness and resilience.

Recap: Building Reactive Resilience

✓ Optimists outperform pessimists in most areas of life and exhibit higher levels of health and longevity.

✓ An optimistic explanatory style (versus a pessimistic one):
  ○ Attributes the cause of bad events to external factors as opposed to internal factors – instead of blaming oneself, we can take responsibility for our contribution to that event, but keep it in proportion by acknowledging other contributing factors.
  ○ Acknowledges that bad events are temporary, as opposed to permanent.
  ○ Acknowledges the situation is specific rather than applying to all aspects of one's life.

✓ Both an optimistic and a pessimistic explanatory style have a time and place, but rewiring your mindset to apply the right one at the right time will enable your resilience and well-being.

✓ While people tend to assume an adversity leads directly to our feelings, it is our thoughts and beliefs about the situation that lead us to develop those feelings.

✓ Combatting disproportionate thoughts, by seeking alternative explanations or finding evidence to support/invalidate our beliefs, is thus a useful way to reclaim control of our feelings and take more appropriate actions.

✓ Identify your most common thinking traps, or cognitive distortions, and create a mental script to combat them. This will allow you to get into a better aligned state of mind faster, and bounce back from the setback more effectively.

✓ Teach your child that if they control their thoughts, they can control their feelings and actions.

✓ When your child shares something that went badly, don't jump right in to solve or judge, ask questions first.
  ○ Legitimise the feeling.
  ○ Ask them to articulate the thoughts that went through .their head during the event.
  ○ Ask them how accurate those thoughts (assumptions) are and what alternative explanations there could be.
  ○ Ask them how they can find the data to prove or

disprove their assumptions.
  o Empower them to act and address the issue by either seeking the evidence, or taking action to correct the situation.
✓ Over time, identify their recurring thinking traps and, at the right age, make them aware to help them identify their own distortions independently in the future.
✓ For a less cerebral way to turn a bad event around, use reset buttons (actions that renew you mentally and physically).
✓ Identify your reset buttons and help your child identify their own, so you can both harness them at the appropriate time.

Section IV

Building Proactive Resilience

So far we have spoken about ways we can react to minimise the impact of adverse situations on both our body and our mind. But there is more we can do to not just be reactive, and instead take charge of building an arsenal of bankable resilience to enable us to thrive.

When my mother was in the final stages of her cancer, I had some of the most dreadful days and paradoxically some of the best days of my life. Whilst I would sit by her side at home and later at the hospital, watching her fade before my eyes, I somehow managed to find things throughout the day to make me feel more alive than I ever had before. And although I felt guilty for those moments where I felt good in spite of her suffering, this was precisely the best medicine for my broken heart.

I had turned to yoga as soon as my mother was diagnosed with cancer, because at the time it was extolled in the US, where I lived at the time of her diagnosis, as something that could aid relaxation. I found the first yoga studio near my house in Philadelphia and walked right into a heated room, where my love affair with hot yoga began. I also found time to introduce things that I loved, such as learning, into our daily routine. I signed up for a long-distance cooking course to make her new three-course meals every day. I took lessons in Mandarin, and I bought financial investment books to help me learn more while she was in bed, sleeping. So far so good, nothing to feel 'guilty' about.

But then when one of my best friends from the University of Pennsylvania came to visit. He introduced me to his friend, who lived in Madrid, with a view to cheering me up. Although I was technically Spanish, I had never lived in Spain, and only moved there when I chose to quit my London job to take care of my mother. I told my friends I had no desire to go out as I wanted to spend every possible minute with my mom. They insisted and said they would wait for me outside the house until my mother had gone to bed for the night. Feeling bad that they were going to all this effort, I decided to go ahead and meet up with them. What followed was the beginning of incredibly intense, fun friendships that led me to experience a wonderful side of Madrid and meet my now husband.

I often felt guilty that I was having a nice time, whilst my mother was sleeping sick in bed. I didn't know it then, but it was precisely what I needed to do to survive those challenging times. After my father's passing, when I became aware of the world of positive psychology, I proactively started to do this. To relish in the fact that, in spite of being in mourning, I had to seek opportunities to maximise happiness and enjoy it in the brief moments it appeared.

So what does positive psychology say about proactively generating and prolonging positive emotion to bank resilience?

10 | The What and Why of Banking Resilience

Social psychologists and positive psychologists like Fredrickson helped develop the *Broaden-and-Build Theory*. This theory postulates that positive emotions – such as love, joy, and gratitude – play an essential role in our survival, inspiring creativity, action, and social ties. The broaden part of this theory relates to the fact that 'when people experience positive emotions, their minds *broaden* and they open up to new possibilities and ideas.' The building part of this theory relates to the fact that 'positive emotions help people *build* their personal well-being resources, ranging from physical resources, to intellectual resources, and social resources.'[22] These resources are considered durable and can be accessed in different emotional states to maintain well-being.

Neuroscience also supports the fact that we can 'bank resilience' by extending and prolonging positive experiences, growing positive neural circuitry in our brains that becomes easier to activate the next time a bad event happens. Rick Hanson explains this process in more detail in his book, *Hardwiring Happiness*. The simplified version of it is that bad memories stick in our brain 'like Velcro' and good ones 'like

[22] Fredrickson, 2009.

Teflon', albeit I prefer the expression that positive memories tend to sift through 'like sand'. When the bad memories stick, it creates larger networks of negative memories, and these become easier for us access. This means a minor bad event can sometimes create an overreaction on our part, because we link it to other bigger bad events and it becomes difficult to handle. However, if we prolong positive experiences in our brain, which is not natural for us given the way we were wired from an evolutionary standpoint, we can create thicker positive neural circuits to tap into when things turn sour. In fact, we can use these more easily accessible memories to short circuit the negative thoughts, and stop them on their tracks. Hanson goes so far as to share techniques to rewire the brain's negative memories all together, by associating them with positive ones to soften the impact of the bad in our memory. It is hard to do his book justice in such little space, so if you're interested in this topic, I can only recommend that you get yourself a copy.

Earlier in the book, we mentioned that the presence of positive emotion is one of the six manifestations of a flourishing person. If this all still sounds a bit fluffy, before we discuss techniques to generate more positive emotion, let me share some hard facts about why building positive emotion matters.

Firstly, generating positive emotion is not automatic, even for people with strong coping skills. We are descended from those who were cautious in caveman times, the ones that believed the rustling behind the bush was not a toddler playing but a lion trying to eat them instead. As reptiles we had to first stay safe, so those that looked out for peril were rewarded with longer lives and more offspring. As a result, our negative circuitry is in play since birth. Rewiring the brain takes time – as we already explained, we have to work to make the good 'stick'. The advantages of generating positive emotion – not just happiness, but calm, contentedness, joy, and peace – are that it broadens awareness and creativity. These enhanced neural circuits make more parts of our brain accessible to us, and allow us to 'connect more dots', which enhance our creativity.

Studies have also shown that positive emotion buffers against depression. People who journal things they are grateful for daily are 30% less likely to exhibit depressive symptoms than people who do not have this habit. Positive emotion also builds resilience. When times get tough, we have more vivid imagery to summon to shorten the negative period. Gratitude, which is a form of generating positive emotion, has also been shown to enhance life satisfaction, and the habit of savouring has been associated with longevity. If that is not enough, appreciation and pointing out others' strengths has shown to improve both individual and team performance.

So what is going on at a neural level when we are generating positive emotion, and how did this come about?

According to Graziano Breuning, in the book *Habits of a Happy Brain*, there are four main 'happy chemicals' (I call them 'happy juices' when speaking with children to keep it simple and fun):

- **Endorphins**. This chemical is segregated when we push our body to experience pain. It is nature's anaesthetic. This chemical helped us ignore pain when we were under attack by a predator, so we could muster the energy to find safety; it also helped us stay numb to pain so we could escape other types of harm. In today's modern world we typically segregate endorphins when we exercise, pushing our heart rate to its maximum. The reason one stops segregating endorphins when one continues to do the same exercise is that once it is no longer arduous, the benefits are gone. Thus one is obliged to keep 'pushing outside the comfort zone' to segregate continued levels of endorphins. For those that exercise regularly, you'll relate to the feeling of being on a high, feeling good about yourself, and realising your problems seem smaller after exercise, which is why you are probably keen that your children exercise too. You may also have experienced the endorphin dip when you don't exercise, which can result in bad moods.

- **Dopamine**. This chemical is segregated when we get what we seek – this could be that piece of chocolate, that promotion, or the finish line after a marathon. It motivates us to get what we need in spite of considerable effort.

From an evolutionary standpoint, this is the chemical that motivated us to walk long distances, and forage or hunt for extended hours to seek food, water, or shelter. When your child throws that tantrum because they want that extra piece of chocolate, or when you feel demotivated after finding out you didn't get the promotion, they/you are experiencing a dopamine dip.

* **Oxytocin**. Also known as the 'love hormone', this chemical is segregated when we are in the comfort of social alliances. Its main evolutionary purpose is to motivate us to trust others so we can find safety in companionship. From an evolutionary standpoint, those of us that stuck to the tribe were more likely to survive. Thus oxytocin is the chemical we segregate when we feel like we belong. People who are used to being the centre of attention, teenagers that want to be popular, or those with FOMO (fear of missing out) are craving this chemical. We can also have oxytocin dips when we feel left out or rejected. Your child may feel this when they find out they did not get invited to a birthday party, or when a friend tells them they don't want to be their friend any more.

* **Serotonin**. Historically, this chemical motivated us to get social respect to enhance the likelihood that we would expand our mating opportunities, guaranteeing our survival and that of our offspring. In the animal kingdom, the alpha males and females had a greater range of mates, allowing them to procreate more frequently and have more offspring. Females wanted to get the highest ranked male to enhance the likelihood that their offspring would survive. In today's society, wherever people have not yet been able to develop their own sense of self-importance, they will seek social respect from others and try to flaunt their status using status symbols. This can drive people to work harder for that corner office, or work longer to make more money, or drive them to want that bigger house no

matter the cost. But it can also be the need or desire to be socially respected and acknowledged as the most popular, get the most attention in a group, or simply to seek work of meaning and social impact. What you seek will be dependent on how you define success. For a child, the feeling of mastering a task, doing something well, or getting praised can elicit this type of chemical reaction.

Endorphins	Dopamine	Oxytocin	Serotonin
Oblivion that masks pain	Joy of finding what you seek	Comfort of social alliances	Security of social importance
Ignore pain so you can escape when injured	Get what you need in spite of a lot of effort	Trust others and find safety in companionship	Get respect to expand your mating opportunities and protect your offspring

So what do we do with this knowledge of chemicals? Firstly, we can look within ourselves to see what habits these chemicals are creating in us. Then we can ask ourselves if these habits are serving us well. If they are, we can choose to keep them, as they are, after all, generating positive emotion for us, which we know is good for us. If we find that an addiction to any of these chemicals is driving us to unreasonable behaviours, such as working our butts off in an office all day, in spite of ample wealth, just to get that promotion without being able to spend any time with our family, we may want to take a step back. At that point we should reassess how else we may be able to 'trick' our brain to either segregate that same hormone differently or to segregate a different happy chemical to break the cycle.

In the case of someone stuck on a serotonin treadmill, linked to external validating events (such as a promotion, a title, an award, etc.), that person may want to spend time redefining success. If success is redefined as 'doing my best every day to provide for my family and spend time with them', then they will get the serotonin kick by simply creating a habit where they look in the mirror and praise themselves for an effort well done that day on the way home at 5 pm as they get to have dinner with the family. I am not suggesting this happens overnight; it is hard work, and figuring out what is important to you in the Aligning Life section should go a long way in helping you do that. But that won't be enough. You'll need clearer goals, and then knowledge of these chemicals and how these addiction loops play a role in your life, to then start thinking creatively about how else to generate them and fill the previous habit void.

How does this apply to your child?

For our kids this has many helpful implications for the following and more:

> **Turning around a mood**: We know if a child is throwing a tantrum, typically one of the basic brain needs (safety, belonging, or mastery), we discussed in the Aligning Mindsets section, is unmet. Their brain is overflowing with cortisol and they may be experiencing an amygdala hijack where all rhyme or reason has left the building. Besides breathing to calm the nervous system and remind the amygdala that it isn't unsafe, excluded or dumb, one can use the above chemicals to counterbalance the cortisol. Here are a few ways one might short circuit the negative-thinking loop and associated negative hormones:
>
> - A hug to segregate oxytocin in the middle of the tantrum
> - A warm word to praise them to segregate serotonin by pointing out the absence of misbehaviour in the middle of poor behaviour ('I can see you controlled yourself this time and didn't throw a pillow, well done')
> - A funny game to jump up and down to segregate

some endorphins
- A moment to let your child read a book/play a quick game/eat a piece of chocolate to segregate dopamine – the key is to find something they like to do and give them time to do it to calm down. Please note I am not endorsing food is used to make feelings good, but this can be helpful in specific situations.

Self-awareness: Children as young as five can understand the idea that these unhappy juices (cortisol) and happy juices (dopamine, oxytocin, serotonin, and endorphins) are segregated inside their brains and bodies, and can affect their mood. This can be eye-opening for some children, especially those interested in how things work.

Self-actualisation: One of my favourite applications of these learnings, however, is that it can teach children that with practice they can control which juices to segregate depending on their actions. Not only will they probably find it quite amusing to think that they can 'control their brain', but it will also empower your child by reinforcing that they can control their thoughts and actions. Understanding the chemicals can give them clues to identify which activities can most effectively change their mood. If they understand that doing exercise segregates endorphins that make them think better (more creatively) and help them feel less anxious (because of the drop in cortisol), they are more likely to want to exercise and stick to it. If you explain to them that wanting that extra piece of chocolate is their brain seeking more dopamine, and that too much chocolate can hurt our tummy, but that they can replace that chemical with oxytocin from a hug, they may look away from food as a way to comfort themselves and replace that with seeking alliances. Giving your children self-awareness and ownership eventually leads to mastery and self-actualisation, building that self-esteem. There are plenty of opportunities to teach these things, usually during or after a tantrum or challenging moment for them, but the trick is staying calm enough ourselves so that we can help our child reason through it all, and asking what helped them after each episode. Over time there will be patterns, and once you've identified and named those patterns, you can turn them into healthy habits.

So what are some techniques to segregate the aforementioned chemicals that we can use for our children and ourselves? Yes, we will need to use plenty of these ourselves to build up the patience – and resilience – to teach our kids this stuff without losing our cool. As a Scottish-born Spanish redheaded mother of two, I know just how hard it is when a little minion is shouting at you as if you were the reason for all their problems, to stay calm enough to help them dissect the issue and turn the mood around. That said, it is the wiring of these networks that will serve them a lifetime. So invest in yourself to be able to invest in your child, and you'll undoubtedly see the benefits – eventually!

11 | Using Savouring to Intensify Positive Emotion

When I first learned about this, it became one of my favourite ways to generate positive emotion. Savouring is mindfully engaging in thoughts or behaviours that heighten the effect of positive events on positive feelings (some just use the shortcut 'mindfulness' to explain savouring in the moment). In other words, savouring is to intensify or prolong a positive experience, thus turning into positive emotion. These emotions can include joy, gratitude, serenity, interest, hope, pride, amusement, inspiration, awe, and love. Savouring can therefore increase positive emotions, but also deepen gratitude (another technique we will discuss), facilitate mindfulness, enhance engagement and meaning.

During our workshops executives shared some of their savouring strategies, which included:

- Taking five minutes between meetings to contemplate favourite photos of loved ones and good memories

- Using the commute home to deliberately think through three things that went well that day that they are thankful for, so that they arrived home relaxed and with a sense of perspective and purpose about their day

- Re-reading thank you notes that clients send them and which they had stored in a 'happy folder' after other clients give them a hard time (to remind them that they do have many wins as well as the odd loss)

In some ways these executives use savouring as a reset button – a way to generate that positive emotion to turn the day around. I must admit that during my corporate career I used a variety of the above techniques, which I picked up along the way thanks to the best managers that crossed my path. This skill served me well as I transitioned into entrepreneurship (where the lows are just as frequent if not more frequent than the wins at the start) and it served me wonders during my father's final stages of cancer when our baby girl was born. I would often try to let the experience of cuddling the little one sink in and make time stand still, to forget just for those twenty minutes that my father was in severe pain in the room next door. To some this may sound morbid, but with the benefit of hindsight I now know this was an instinctive and accurate survival strategy and I was banking resilience for what was to come.

So, what are some parameters we can keep in mind to savour more often?

Savouring can be done at three distinct times:

- Before an event – anticipating the positive experiences you will have

- During an event – codifying and mindfully engaging in the experience

- After an event – reminiscing, sharing past experience

Maybe you have a friend who buys a travel guide before going somewhere, plans exactly what they will do and relishes the thought of discussing their upcoming holiday? This person is savouring before the event. You may also have gone on holiday with the type that loves taking pictures, takes the time to soak in the scenery, the food and the views, constantly showers you with positive commentary on the experience and can't stop smiling throughout? That's savouring in the moment. Perhaps you also have a friend who invites people over after a holiday to show them their pictures? This is an example of savouring after the event.

A modern twist on savouring that has been overused to the point of making others feel bad is the so-called 'holiday spam' on social media platforms like Instagram. Used effectively, these can be great ways to savour, codify, and allow you to 'past' savour great events. (I use my personal Instagram account this way, and during a rainy day can go back to my pictures to relive holiday highlights and instantly feel better). Whatever you choose to incorporate into your life, all these techniques are equally valid, and together they represent a huge opportunity to codify and hardwire far more positive emotion than if you otherwise just travelled to the destination, took a few photos, and then came back home to resume your normal routine.

Savouring can also happen in different dimensions, which my fellow INSEAD MBAs-turned-consultants reading this will relish – the famous 2x2 matrix at its best.

On one axis is the focus of attention, which can be external or internal, and on the other axis is the type of experience, which can be mental (cognitive reflection) or physical (experiential absorption).[23]

---

[23] Bryant and Veroff, 2007.

	Focus of Attention: Internal Self	Focus of Attention: External World
Type of Experience: Cognitive Reflection	**Basking** pride: receptive to praise and congratulations	**Thanksgiving** gratitude: experiencing and expressing gratitude
Type of Experience: Experiential Absorption	**Luxuriating** pleasure: engaging the senses fully	**Marveling** awe: losing self in wonder of the experience

If you reflect on how well you delivered a killer presentation, you'll probably notice the feeling of pride. Basking in that glory, internally, is just one way of enhancing the positive experience of that presentation. Guess the effect that will have next time you go and present? Yes, it will create positive associations that you can more easily draw on if you're nervous and have to remind yourself that things you care about are at stake.

If, on the other hand, you decide to share those feelings outwardly during the meeting, you may start to feel gratitude. Thank the organisers for a good event, a receptive audience, perfect logistics, etc. This will not only make you feel good but those around you too. Once again, you'll magnify the experience.

Perhaps you've taken a bubble bath and enjoyed the warmth against your skin, and the soothing effect the lower lighting has on your eyes. That would be you luxuriating. Finally, you may be travelling through Roman temples in Italy, taking in all the sights, marvelling at the incredible things past civilisations could build without modern technology. These again are savouring techniques you can draw upon. Just by becoming aware of them, you will be better able to make use of the techniques to generate positive feelings. There are plenty other ways you can savour, and here are just a few:

Technique	What it is
Sharing with others	Seeking others to share experiences and memories
Memory building	Actively storing images for future recall, taking mental photographs, and forming vivid images
Self-congratulation	Cognitive basking, telling self how proud or impressed you/others are in response to achievements and personal success
Comparing	Contrasting your own feelings with what others are feeling, comparing to past experiences
Sensory perceptual sharpening	Intensifying pleasure by focusing on certain stimuli and screening out others, concentration, positive vigilance, slowing down
Absorption	Mindfulness without cognitive reflection
Temporal awareness	Reminding self how fleeting the moment is, telling oneself that one must enjoy
Counting blessings	Acknowledging gratitude

How does this apply to your child?

It has been shown kids will typically mimic their parents or primary caretaker. Thus, merely expressing awe, thanksgiving, or relish will help your children to do the same. Explaining to kids the advantages of making themselves happy by generating positive thoughts is just the beginning. Setting an example for how one can savour is the vehicle through which you can help them attain this. Ultimately though, your children will see the advantages, because they will *feel* them. In fact, because children have more mirror neurons, they are able to experience the positive emotion just by seeing you experience it, activating the positive emotion regions of the brain simultaneously.

Being around someone that savours, and savours out loud, is also extremely pleasant and generates feelings of happiness for those around too. So imagine the positivity you can spread by teaching your children to do this and how they can inspire their friends to do the same. Parents can often be heard saying 'be grateful for what you have', but rarely express that out loud themselves, and savouring is just one way of showcasing how to do that. I'm certain you'll start to see the benefits of this in both your and your children's moods in no time, creating a healthy addiction to the happy juices that savouring can help you all segregate. Here is a thought exercise to get you started:

Exercise IX: Savouring

Take a look at the list of savouring techniques we have discussed in this chapter.

Self-Reflection: What savouring techniques do I use most and least? What techniques would I like to incorporate more into my life?

Depending on their age, take a moment to show some of these techniques to your child. If they are too young, imagine what their answers might be.

Discussion: What techniques does my child use most? What techniques would they like to use more?

Depending on your child's age, you may do the following as a family or with your partner.

Discussion: What family routines can you create to savour more often?

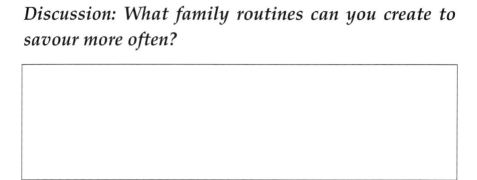

Now let's take a look at one more savouring technique that is also a significant social skill. I like to call this tool **savouring together**, but scientists have a more accurate name for it: **active constructive responding (ACR).** This tool was developed by psychologists to show the optimal way of responding to someone when they share good news with you. Their research shows that one of the biggest predictors of relationships' durability and strength is what friends do when things are going well for us. In fact, the closest, most intimate, and most trusting relationships appear to be distinguished not by how the partners respond to each other's disappointments and losses, but how they react to good news.[24]

Ask yourself this question: How did you react the last time a friend told you they were promoted? Or they told you they wrote a book? Or your child told you they moved up to a harder maths group? Or your son said he drew an elaborate picture at school? If you're like most people, you possibly said 'Great news, good for you.' While this is a perfectly acceptable way to respond, it is missing a beat. It misses the invitation to help that person savour and turn their positive experience into a positive emotion.

Following are four alternative ways a person can typically react, and the best possible way to do so from a scientific standpoint is the top left hand quadrant:[25]

---

[24] Lyubomirsky, 2010.

[25] Gable, et al., 2004.

	Constructive	Destructive
Active	**Enthusiastic Support** (e.g. 'That's great news. How did you find out?')	**Negating the Positive** (e.g. 'Oh that will be a lot of work.')
Passive	**Quiet, Understated Support** (e.g. 'Great.')	**Ignoring the Event** (e.g. 'Oh, by the way I found your hat.')

By asking your friend, partner, or child more about the situation and how they feel, you're inviting them to talk about the details of what happened, and turn their 'great' feelings into a stronger emotion. It is also an excellent opportunity for them to verbalise the strengths they may have been putting to good use to achieve those things.

As we will later find out, being aware of and using our strengths is yet another way to generate positive emotion. What you may also notice is that when you invite someone else to savour, you'll see that they are happier and it will make you happier in turn, activating your evolutionary altruistic circuits. So responding constructively to people in general will not only help you help them, but it will help you too. Let's face it, this is a terrific social skill for young children to learn (and adults to apply) in order to build and deepen relationships quickly.

Exercise X: Transforming Relationship Dynamics

This simple exercise can turn around broken dynamics. If you've found yourself being overly negative with your child, this is an easy way to turn their mood around, and help them associate speaking with you to the generation of positive emotion – quickly.

How can you adopt a more active constructive stance?

1) First identify which relationships you'd like to strengthen

2) Then identify the way you typically respond to that person

3) Next, ask yourself what you'd like to enhance

4) Then identify how you would like to respond next time

Person	Situation	My usual response	My active constructive response
Identify a relationship that you would like to strengthen	*Identify a typical good news situation*	*Identify a response that you would like to enhance*	*Identify how you would like to respond*

12 | Harnessing the Power of Expressions of Gratitude

Gratitude is our sense of thankfulness, appreciation, and joy for the good things in our life. On our savouring 2x2, this resided in the axis where focus on the external world and cognitive reflection met.

Intentionally expressing gratitude enhances our daily positive emotion and overall life satisfaction. This is because gratitude amplifies our awareness of the good things in our lives, increasing the frequency and intensity of our positive thoughts, feelings, and memories.

Exactly how gratitude works for us depends on our individual disposition, life circumstances, and the thing we are feeling grateful for. Here are just some of the ways that expressing gratitude can help us:

- Expressing gratitude can help us cope with stress and trauma

- Expressing gratitude displaces negative emotions (e.g. it is hard to feel grateful and angry at the same time)

- Expressing gratitude encourages kinder behaviours because we have a more positive view of those around us

- Expressing gratitude can strengthen our existing relationships and help us to nurture new ones because we feel more connected to others, and this can create an 'upward spiral' between our feelings towards others and our interactions with them

- Expressing gratitude tends to inhibit counterproductive comparison with others

- Expressing gratitude can help us overcome 'hedonic adaptation', our automatic tendency to adjust to the good things in our life so that they are 'priced in' to the way we experience our world

We have already discussed why expressing gratitude takes effort at first. Our ancestors planned for the worst, rather than relishing the best, to enhance their likelihood of survival. So in those ancient times, gratitude actually had high costs. But these days, physical and environmental threats are less relevant, and so focusing on the negative can make us anxious in ways that are counterproductive. Gratitude can give us a path out of counterproductive worrying.

As well as the emotional and relationship benefits, some studies have even shown that gratitude and other positive emotions can boost our physical health. For example, people who participated in a gratitude journaling exercise reported fewer physical symptoms (e.g. headaches, acne, coughing) than control groups, and spent more time exercising.

At a corporate level there are also significant advantages that are well documented in performance lift due to higher levels of engagement and closer friendships. At an anecdotal level, I lived its benefits working at CEB, a best practices research firm that, when I joined was valued at $300 million, before later being sold to Gartner for $2 billion – it was the 'belle of Wall Street' for a number of years. CEB was relentless in its pursuit of results in the most engaging of ways. Instead of hiring the most blue chip education accredited individuals (though there were many there), it focused on four things during recruitment: fire in the belly, firm citizenship, member service, and spirit of generosity. In this way, CEB recruited incredibly ambitious people that also knew how to be nice, kind, thoughtful, and grateful. I am confident that played a huge role in our team's success. We celebrated each other's wins, expressed our gratitude individually and as a group, and created intense friendships. In fact, it is no surprise to me that after people departed CEB, they variously went to places where other CEBers resided, went to work for other CEB managers, married a CEB colleague, or continued to stay lifelong friends.

How does this apply to your child?

Similarly to savouring, setting an example by expressing gratitude is key. For example, after learning about the benefits of expressing gratitude and explaining that to my kids (ages five and seven) in layman's terms – 'Being grateful will make you happier and those around you too; being happier will make your brain grow as it will be more creative' – we proceeded to establish a family habit at dinner time. When we sit around the table, we each have to report one thing that went well that day that we are grateful for, one thing that did not go well (so we can learn to problem-solve together), one person we were kind to, and one person that was kind to us. This simple exercise helps the children, and us, to remind ourselves of things that went well, that we are grateful for, and also immediately makes us feel grateful for having the support network we have created for each other at home.

We also are regularly in the habit of discussing the three things we are grateful for after the kids have been tucked into bed. Talking about these right before bedtime can dispel any cortisol related to last-minute pre-bed worries, and it can also help your child have better, happier dreams, as they go down to sleep with 'happy juices' coursing through their brains. Not to mention how amazing you will feel at hearing what your children are grateful for.

I've found this to be an illuminating exercise in getting to know what my children value, and how different those things can be. Often they correspond to a personal interest, the happy chemicals they crave, or the things they pay attention to. For example, my daughter will typically bring up moments where she has either had a good time with a friend, had a cuddle from me/her dad, or had a laugh with her brother. She is an oxytocin junkie that loves enjoying things with people. My son, on the other hand, will typically talk about how he solved a harder maths problem today than yesterday, how he was proud that he controlled his temper when he didn't make the football team this week, or how much he enjoyed running around at break time. He is a serotonin and endorphin junkie. He loves to feel mastery and loves to exercise.

The above gives me valuable clues. Next time they are throwing a tantrum I can use techniques that will help them segregate the chemicals they crave most through action. For my daughter, it is giving her a hug, lots of warm praise, or doing something together, and for my son it is either kicking the football around, or reminding him of how far he has come along controlling his 'downstairs brain' to help him feel mastery. Believe it or not, this has become the crux of our parenting toolkit at home, and it was all because through these gratitude exercises, my husband and I identified what they valued most. Whilst what they value may change over time, and I am by no means claiming to have cracked the system, I am hopeful that sharing my personal experience may help spark some ideas in you that are better suited to your parenting style and family routine.

Here are some exercises to help you reflect on what may work for you.

Exercise XI: Incorporating Gratitude

Take a stab at these questions:

Self-Reflection: How can I incorporate more gratitude into my everyday life?

```



```

Take a moment to discuss the importance of expressing gratitude to your child. Then, as a family, consider the following:

Discussion: What family routines can we create to incorporate more gratitude into our lives?

```



```

Exercise XII: Gratitude Journal

The purpose of this exercise is to enable you to increase your well-being through the deliberate cultivation of gratitude.

This week, and for as many as you can continue to do so (aim for a minimum of thirty days straight), set aside a few minutes to 'step outside' your life and thoughtfully reflect on the things that went well each day.

Write down **three things** that went well and **why** they went well. Write them somewhere you can refer to a later date, should you wish.

The things you express gratitude for need not be earth-shaking in importance ('the electrician came and fixed the lights today' or, 'my husband and I had a lovely dinner together on Wednesday' or, 'I am grateful for the compliment my friend gave me today'), but they can be important too ('my cousin told me that she loved me' or, 'my childhood friend gave birth to a healthy baby').

In each case, identify why the good thing happened ('my husband and I had a lovely dinner together because I suggested we go out for a change, and he arranged his schedule to arrive early' or, 'the electrician came and fixed the lights today because I remembered to call and arrange it, even though I was so busy this week'). You may decide to include a few 'big picture' items too ('I am grateful for my family' or, 'I am grateful that I have reached this point in my career').

Expressing gratitude in this way may seem awkward at first, but stick with it and adapt the exercise if needed so that it feels authentic. The odds are that you will quite quickly learn to enjoy it and, before you know it, you'll start looking forward to it as a way to write a happy ending to your day.

Next Level

- Although on average this exercise tends to have the biggest impact when done daily, you may decide to do it more or less frequently depending on what suits your lifestyle and disposition. You may even opt to do it only when you need a boost or when you have a bad day. The important thing is to find a way that works best for you.

- Don't forget the specific individuals who care for you, or have somehow touched your life. Thinking of people we are close to can trigger oxytocin and also gratitude for many of the best things in our lives.

- Once you have had a bit of practice, you may choose to make the exercise 'social'. Many people have found that the exercise works especially well with partners and children as part of your routine. Others prefer to take a less structured approach, but deliberately take a few opportunities each week to express gratitude in ways that they might not previously have done. Some even exchange journals with friends via messaging apps, or use the journal as a way of looking back on their month with friends and family. You could even choose to use your Instagram or another social media platform account, as a pictorial gratitude journal equivalent.

13 | Unearthing and Capitalising on Your Strengths

This is one of my favourite management techniques. During my time at Egon Zehnder assessing C-suite executives across leadership competencies, we would often find that leaders lacked the ability to 'build organisational capability', a competency that entails managing people in a way that foments individual and organisational success. People who are skilled in this competency often find satisfaction in influencing or even transforming someone's life or career. They typically take pride in effectively making themselves redundant, helping their people develop and outgrow them. This competency is essential to leadership success, and can often set superb individual contributors with potential to reach leadership and executive ranks apart from the rest. This competency entails a number of skills, as follows:

- *Diagnoses individual and team capability:*

  - Showing awareness of self and individual colleagues' strengths and development needs

  - Showing awareness of how the team is working (and how it could work better)

- *Acts as coach:*

  - Building positive emotion through recognition, praise, and curious questions

  - Providing growth feedback

  - Creating a safe learning environment

  - Cultivating a sense of meaning in work, explaining how team members contribute to the effectiveness and impact of the team to drive behavioural change

  - Enabling achievement by harnessing individual strengths

- *Champions talent management:*

  - Recruiting the best people for the role/organisation

  - Identifying strengths and maximising them in the context of the team and organisation

  - Helping develop and mentor beyond the team

  - Helping promote

  - Helping explore options outside the firm when relevant

  - Identifying successors for each role and encouraging talent mobility internally and externally where applicable

You'll see that these skills are plain common sense, but they are easier written than done. And in fact, a lot of managers think of their job as just guiding a team to the right outcomes without focusing on *how* they get to those outcomes. Research in the field of positive psychology has made one thing clear – focusing on developing people's strengths pays dividends. Strengths-based managers are more effective than non-strengths-based managers, and employees working for strengths-based managers are less likely to quit and six times more likely to be engaged at work.

Research by Rath and Conchie on strengths-based leadership and focus says that workers whose managers primarily focus on their strengths have only a 1% chance of being actively disengaged at work, compared to an over 20% chance for those workers whose managers primarily focus on their weaknesses. One reason why leading through strengths promotes higher performance is that exercising our strengths boosts our self-confidence – whereas focusing on our weaknesses undermines it – promoting higher performance, job satisfaction, income, and even improved physical health.[26] One CEO of a global bank summarised the need for leaders to promote strengths-based cultures more concisely, saying that leaders needed to have 'a positive bias', because employees 'don't want to follow negative people around').[27]

If knowing that focusing on strengths could be your ticket to the C-suite, what if I then told you that focusing on strengths can make our children more resilient, healthier, and happier? Focusing on strengths will also help your child identify their own so they can experience more 'flow' in their lives as they grow up – i.e. more Engagement (the E in PERMAS). We already established that at a young age children flow by playing – their strengths are to learn through play. But as they get older, focusing on identifying their strengths can bring a huge competitive advantage, as well as a source of energy and happiness.

So how can you help your child identify their strengths if you don't know your own? The first step is for you to get in the habit of identifying your own. But there is a problem. We are often unaware of our strengths because we are 'unconsciously competent'. If we've been praised emptily for most of our lives without much explanation as to what we are doing well, then we are incapable of building organisational (or in this case self)

---

[26] Judge and Hurst, 2008; Rath and Conchie, 2008.

[27] Rath and Conchie, 2008.

capability. The learning process tends to go something like this·

STEP 1: Unconscious Incompetence

STEP 2: Conscious Incompetence

STEP 3: Conscious Competence

STEP 4: Unconscious Competence

1. We are unconsciously incompetent – we do not know what we do not know

2. We become consciously incompetent – we become aware of what we do not know

3. We become consciously competent – as we learn the skills to learn whatever we are trying to do

4. Once we have become good at something, we become unconsciously competent – we do not know why we do what we do so well, we just 'do it'

When you strengths spot, you are helping someone go from Step 4 to Step 3. Other ways to become aware of your strengths include becoming a student again, reading a book that will teach you how to improve, or observing someone who is good at what you want to do. But there are also ways you can help your children grow, taking them from Step 4 to Step 3 at the appropriate time. Delivering feedback is one of the most difficult skills to develop and one that few people are gifted at. If the purpose of feedback is to create behavioural change (be it by encouraging more good behaviour or eliminating poor behaviour), then feedback should be descriptive, precise, timely, and actionable.

Often parents are competent at timely, but they may fall short of descriptive and precise. Some of our parents may have just said 'well done' when we brought them a pretty picture, missing both an opportunity to react more constructively by helping us to savour our task together and expand the positive emotion, as well as missing an opportunity to tell us what was good about our picture so we can build upon that and tweak whatever will improve it further. Some of us may have had parents that didn't praise outcomes per se but praised process instead – and told us things like, 'I love the way you paid close attention by looking at me in the eye, focused on what I was saying, and waited until I was finished before responding. Then you asked a clarifying question to make sure you understood – that is what I call active listening.' These parents would have not only praised you and made you feel good about yourself, generating positive emotion, but they would have also taught you what active listening is, how to demonstrate it, and that you're actually pretty good at it for now. This would have been likely to motivate you to continue to listen closely in the future. Most of us, however, didn't have parents like these – even the best intentioned of them may have never had parents like that themselves, never been formally taught to manage, never became teachers (as teachers are often taught to do this as part of their toolkit), or simply never had the time or the inclination to use these techniques.

Using a clear descriptive praising process (and focusing on process not outcome) is a gift that will take your child from unconsciously competent to consciously competent, which is exactly how they can teach what they know to others as they grow. Plant this seed and watch your children become masters at praising and encouraging their friends, and turning into natural leaders, managers and people developers when they grow up. This seed you plant may just be their ticket to their desired position of leadership, and at minimum be at the heart of their source of strength and confidence for years to come. This will be the beginning of their strengths psychology mindset – one that focuses on others' strengths and celebrates them, generating positive emotions for all.

So what is the technique?

When praising:

- Pick the right time –usually straight after the event has taken place is best

- Pick the right tone – get down to their level, look them in the eye, and try to transmit energy by smiling to make the experience even more intense

- Pick the right words – state specific action(s)/behaviour(s) they demonstrated, and how you were able to observe it by describing the facts around it

- Teach impact – describe the impact it had on you/the person in question and how it probably made that person feel

This technique will generate not only oxytocin, but also dopamine and serotonin. It invites the child to savour, lets the good chemicals sink in, and expands strengths by motivating them to do more of it (seeking more of that happy high). It will deepen 'strengths psychology': children's ability to notice the strengths of others and create more positive thinking patterns.

This can also be a super useful and fun family exercise. Over dinner, try a strengths-spotting exercise where each member of the family has to state one thing each person in the family excels in. Watch people smile as they hear the feedback, and watch each of you develop precise, observant praising skills. You'll also notice that you will start to pay more attention to what you each do well. It can also be an effective antidote to sibling rivalry, by asking siblings to praise each other, or highlighting things each sibling is great at to offset any feelings of jealousy and reinforce the altruistic circuits.

As mentioned earlier, altruistic joy is within our inherited neural circuitry. Our ancestors lived in small bands in which individuals had to work together through tough times to keep the children alive. The ability to take joy and pleasure in the success of others helped to foster stronger bonds, enhancing the likelihood that genes were passed on. Feeling happiness for others is thus an inclination of the human heart and an opportunity to let the good sink into your brain, moulding neural circuits to focus on the good, and enhancing your resilience. Thus, when a sibling does something wonderful, take the time to praise the strengths deliberately, and teach your child that feeling pride in the success of others is part of their circuitry.

Whilst children's personalities aren't formed until the ages of sixteen to eighteen (research on this varies, but it is roughly around the end of adolescence and the beginning of young adulthood), you can use strengths spotting as a way to identify emerging preferences, likes and dislikes, and affinities/early budding abilities.

Exercise XIII: Strengths Spotter

The following can be a helpful exercise to identify your own strengths. Be as specific as possible.

Self-Reflection: Describe a situation where you have been at your best, and identify what strengths you used.

```



```

You may want to ask your child to do their own version. You'll be surprised how young they can start to formulate answers. The mere fact that you ask the question will help steer them to start thinking about strengths as a general mindset.

You may want to take the above one step further, and take a diagnostic questionnaire to identify your strengths in a more quantifiable way – or at least in a way that allows you to compare your results relative to others. Most can be helpful to generate thinking, and I am always a believer in simple is best if you're doing it yourself.

In our workshops we use Martin Seligman's VIA (virtues in action) survey. It is free, and the sample size is vast so the reliability of the data and relevance is sound. There is also wonderful research behind it and lots to be learned about oneself when you take the online questionnaire. If you'd like to take yours, go to https://www.viacharacter.org/survey/account/register.

Whilst personality is not formed well into, and sometimes past, the teenage years, children as young as seven can take the VIA strengths with parental support to start exploring, and as a point of departure for conversations. It is important that the results are not used to label or categorise yourself or your child.

In fact, these should be used merely as a conversation starter to help you and your child explore what makes them feel strong. In 3VERS executive alignment sessions, however, we use 16PF, a traits-based questionnaire, that provides the basis for a more nuanced discussion. The psychometric measures how much of each of the sixteen distinct personality factors you possess. Everyone has all sixteen, but we each have them to different degrees, signalling our preference(s). With each trait there are associated strengths and weaknesses, and the exploration of their various combinations can make for a deeply profound and unique analysis of yourself and your more intrinsic rather than extrinsic motivations. I would not recommend this tool for a person under the age of eighteen, but I highly recommend you get in touch if you would like to explore ways to use this tool to garner self-insight as an adult.

14 | Embrace the Bottom of the Iceberg: MEDS

Thus far we've talked about many tools that can serve both as reset buttons and as resilience buffers. If ABC thinking is the tip of the iceberg when it comes to developing mental toughness, MEDS is the solid foundation underneath the water. It encompasses the daily effort, habits, and routines that people do not often see, but that provide a solid strong base from which to truly flourish. Taking as much care with these four dimensions as with our mental health, and sticking to them as diligently as you do to your daily tooth brushing, is essential to sustaining a flourishing life.

What does MEDS stand for? It's not medication, if that's what you were thinking! Instead it is **M**editation, **E**xercise, **D**iet, and **S**leep. These things, which seem so basic because most of us have already heard about their importance, are often the elements we let slide right out of our routines. Because we are already busy with work, kids, school, and friends, we often leave little time to take care of our basic needs. Without this though, and as well-known social blogger moms say, 'you can't pour from an empty cup'. One must take care of one's basic needs before one can truly thrive, not just in our social, family, and work life, but also within ourselves.

After my mother's passing, I realised that life had a different meaning and that I needed to align my life to those motivations, find my strengths, figure out where they could be helpful, and start to use them. My journey through a series of jobs brought me closer to discovering that, as I went from banking at JP Morgan, consulting at Accenture, leading commercial teams at CEB, an MBA at INSEAD, to recruitment at Egon Zehnder, and lead talent for a global philanthropy. It was after having my second child here that my father was diagnosed with cancer. At this stage, I was juggling a global job, a toddler, a newborn baby, a happy marriage, and a healthy social life. Every waking moment not at work, I was with my children, trying to juggle this superhuman expectation I had to be able to be both my mother and father wrapped into one.

After my dad died whilst managing four different companies with unprecedented levels of stress, I had a stark realisation: I spent zero time on myself. I had been neglecting my basic needs: *actively* taking care of my health. I didn't want this to come back and nip me in the bud. I wanted (and very much still want) to be alive when my kids had their kids and to ensure my children would not have to live through what I did – having children without their mom to help them.

In some ways, starting to apply MEDS into my life forced me to make stark choices. It forced me to realise that to be the mother *I* wanted to be, I needed to create space for me, and that would need to eat away from my work life. That said, I always wanted professional stimulation and had been raised to need that (serotonin and dopamine junkie right here). So I turned to entrepreneurship as my answer, with MEDS as my vehicle to nurse my mental health back to full strength. To this day, I actively keep MEDS in my daily routine. I have been known to turn down interesting jobs, projects, and clients that would take my time away from this. While I recognise I am in a privileged position to be able to choose to do this, I bring it up to point out its importance. Time for MEDS needs to be carved out of existing goals unless it becomes explicit in our goal hierarchies either as a means goal to flourishing or as the ongoing end goal.

However you decide to incorporate MEDS, let's take a look at its importance in more detail. There are many expert practitioners in each of these fields, but I hope to point you in the right direction to learning more and, at minimum, give you basic insights into why each one is important.

Meditation

We've all heard about meditation. It is the new buzzword – mindfulness, meditation, living in the NOW – these are all ways to speak about it. It's a buzz for a reason: it actually works. But not always in the way we think it does. In fact, research is rather mixed in this area.

What most researchers agree on is that meditation increases density of brain tissue, regulates the hippocampus, releases serotonin, GABA, melatonin, lowers cortisol levels, and that it can enhance focus. What researchers differ on, though, is how long and how permanent these effects are. In their book *Altered Traits*, Daniel Goleman and Richard J. Davidson break down meditators into three groups: those dabbling, those with a regular mediation practice (including at least one Vipassana – usually a ten-day silent meditation retreat – in their lifetime), and those for whom it is a way of life (Buddhist monks or advanced yoginis). Their research shows that unless practised regularly, the benefits of meditation disappear. So whilst meditating for ten days straight will likely see a reduction on your stress levels, regulation of the hippocampus, release of GABA and other chemicals that help you sleep, once you stop, the advantages disappear. It isn't until one falls into the third category that actual traits and the brain structure are permanently changed. That said, what the research does validate is that with a regular practise of ten minutes a day, we can start to see benefits from meditation. Creating a habit around it is just as important, as otherwise dabbling in and out will have little to no impact into your long term well-being.

Exercise

Getting enough exercise is also essential to developing resilience. Although most of us know that we can benefit from physical activity, over half of the population regards themselves as inactive.

Research shows that short periods of exercise in the morning can contribute to higher energy levels, which in turn help regulate our sleep. Moderate and *regular* exercise, for example a ten-minute brisk walk, decreases cortisol levels and can reduce anxiety. Exercise has also been shown to make our brain more plastic, and thus enhance our ability to learn. While there is much confusion and mixed research out there on what types of exercise are best, most studies agree that a mixture of cardiovascular, strength training, and restorative stretching exercise such as yoga or Pilates, are the trifecta of a healthy exercise routine. When we exercise we segregate endorphins, which can make us feel good immediately, and as we mentioned earlier, many people use exercise as a reset button. Overall, exercise can boost our cognitive performance. It is no surprise that people with big events, presentations, or working towards something will often choose to exercise to kick-start their day.

The American College of Sports Medicine (ACSM) suggests adults need a mix of physical activity to stay healthy:

- Engage in moderate intensity aerobic activity (anything that gets your heart rate working a bit faster than normal) five days a week between 150 minutes and five hours.

- If you prefer vigorous-intensity aerobic activity such as running, aim for at least seventy-five minutes a week.

- Engage in muscle strengthening activity at least two days a week.

- Consider breaking up longer exercise sessions into three ten-minute shorter sessions in one day if the above is too challenging to fit into your routine at this stage. Even a little bit of exercise if the above is too much still has its health benefits.

The ACSM also recommends three types of suggested exercise:

- *Resistance Exercise* – adults should engage in resistance training two to three days a week.

- *Flexibility Exercise* – adults should conduct this type of exercise at least two to three days a week

- *Neuromotor Exercise* – adults should engage in this type of activity, which includes yoga and Tai Chi, for twenty to thirty minutes a day.[28]

---

[28] Hefferon, 2013.

Diet

'You can't work towards happiness if your brain's machinery isn't well oiled and firing on all cylinders.'[29]

Our diet meets our basic reward needs, and impacts physical and mental performance. A healthy diet can prevent diseases and enhance performance. It can help regulate our sleep, ability to learn, and our moods. As Kate Hefferon puts it in her book, *Positive Psychology and the Body*, 'In order for us to function physically, cognitively and emotionally, we need to make sure that we are ingesting the optimal properties so that we better prepare our body and brain for sustainable change.'[30]

During cortisol peaks, or stressful times, people tend to reach for processed, high-carb, high-sugar foods. While this may satisfy your dopamine cravings in the short term, it can negatively impact your overall health and therefore resilience. Instead, adhering to a **Mediterranean diet**, which includes lots of fruits, omega 3 fatty acids, vegetables, nuts, legumes, fish, and whole grains, and limits red meat and refined sugar, is deemed best. Studies by Sofi et al. found that following this diet significantly reduced risk of 'overall mortality, cardiovascular disease, cancer incidence and mortality and incidence of Parkinson's and Alzheimer's disease.'[31]

Although research in this area varies, most experts agree that an excess of **sugar** is harmful for us. Some studies have shown that there is a 'highly significant correlation' between sugar consumption and the annual rate of depression. While the studies have some limitations, what is true and worrisome is that our sugar consumption has risen dramatically since the sixteenth century when it was first introduced in the UK.

That said, **chocolate**, one of my favourite foods, utilised

---

[29] Graham and Ramsey, 2011.

[30] Hefferon, 2013.

[31] Sofi et al., 2008.

broadly by the Mayan and Aztec civilisations, can be beneficial Today less healthy proliferations are at the centre of many household child-led tantrums, but research now shows that consumption of 100 g/day of dark chocolate has many benefits including enhanced cognition and 'reduced cancer, diabetes, [and] cardiovascular disease'. Other benefits include lowering blood pressure, blood sugar, and cortisol, and improving how we process sugar.[32] Thus there may be no harm in reaching for that tablet of dark 70%+ chocolate; however, it is important not to use it as an antidepressant or to stabilise moods.

A consumption of **carbohydrates**, although contentious amongst experts, has been linked to better mood and higher energy, less anger, anxiety, and depression.[33] Consumption of **omega 3** also bullet proofs against depression and has been linked to neuronal growth, enhanced mood, reduced heart disease and the delay of dementia. Besides fish, ingesting flax seeds or fish oil tablets can also provide much-needed omega 3. Finally, consuming vitamins **A**, **B6**, **B12**, **C**, **D**, and **E**, as well as **folic acid**, **iron**, **zinc**, **copper**, and **selenium**, can boost our immune system.[34]

Finally, we cannot end the section on diet without mentioning **hydration**. We are able to ingest water through drink and food: the latter typically provides 20% of our daily intake. The intake of water and maintenance of hydration is imperative for our physical and psychological functioning. Research shows that losing 2% of our body weight due to water restriction, heat or significant exercise can significantly impair our physical and cognitive performance[35] (how is that for ensuring your child knows the importance of filling up their water bottle at school each day and finishing it?). The Institute of Medicine

---

[32] Graham and Ramsay, 2011.

[33] Benton and Donohue, 1999.

[34] Hefferon, 2013.

[35] Hefferon, 2013.

recommends that children up to the age of nine should ingest up to 800 ml per day. Edmonds and Burford[36] found improved attention and memory in children that are hydrated versus children who aren't. Investing in that all-important school water bottle, labelling it appropriately, and encouraging your child to drink each day could go a long way in enhancing their cognition (and the same goes for you).

A note on 'adult drinks' may also be appropriate here. **Coffee** and **caffeine** have had mixed reviews but recent studies show that caffeine consumption in the right dosage (3-6 mg) at the right time (approximately thirty minutes before you need it), can boost performance. Ideally, caffeine should be used as a tool and not a crutch, and it should be avoided in the afternoons so as to avoid a delay in our ability to sleep.

Alcohol is another contentious element. While many studies have shown drinking wine with tannins at night can help put us to sleep, others have proven exactly the opposite. Most studies agree, however, that if alcohol is ingested, it must be done in moderation to prevent physical and psychological decline. That said, the savouring and social component dimensions of enjoying a small glass of wine may psychologically offset the physiological damage that it can produce. Drink at your own risk, and know that the latest research extols abstinence (don't shoot the messenger, please).

---

[36] Edmonds and Burford, 2009.

Sleep

Research shows that lack of sleep is costing the UK $40 billion in productivity loss, $411 billion in the US, and $138 billion in Japan alone. Employees managed by leaders who sleep less than seven hours per night on average, find their managers to be uninspiring and poor decision-makers in comparison to days where their managers have slept consistently well. Sleep-deprived employees are more error prone, get sicker more often, and make poorer decisions. Imagine the combination of a sleep-deprived manager and a sleep-deprived employee! Go no further; ask yourself if you get enough sleep. In today's society where lights have lit up our nights, our body's circadian rhythms have been completely thrown off. Bear in mind our ancestors were naturally told when to go to sleep and wake with the setting and rising of the sun. What does this mean for us today?

Our sleep and our well-being are closely intertwined. As Matthew Walker, author of *Why We Sleep,* puts it, 'Sleep dispenses a multitude of health-ensuring benefits, yours to pick up in repeat prescription every twenty-four hours, should you choose'. Getting enough high-quality sleep helps us 'learn, memorise, and make logical decisions and choices'. Sleep boosts our mood and ability to concentrate the next day. It also helps us resolve problems, since our brains process new information and experiences while we sleep.

Sleep rids our bodies of toxins, cleanses our immune system, and helps us process difficult situations and emotions. When we wake, our brain has rid itself of unnecessary circuits and connected the required new ones, giving us plenty of energy to meet psychological challenges head on with cool-headed composure (an engaged upstairs and downstairs brain). In the long term, sleep improves our health prospects and resistance to diseases. It also regulates our appetite, helping control body weight. The list goes on and on. Walker puts it best when he says, 'We are now forced to wonder whether there are any biological functions that do not benefit by a good night's sleep. So far ... thousands of studies insist that no, there aren't.'

So what can we do to enhance our sleep? Our sleep is affected by our environment (e.g. light, noise), our deliberate behaviours (e.g. diet, evening routine), and our unique psychology and physiology. While the picture is complex, here is a simplified checklist to help you find your own formula to get enough high-quality sleep.

Sleep Checklist

During the day:

✓ **Do aerobic exercise several times a week:** Aerobic exercise has been shown to increase sleep quality and time (please note anaerobic exercise, such as lifting weights, has been shown to have the opposite effect). If you exercise early in the morning in sunlight, it is recommended you wear sunglasses, and then aim to take a light walk outside in the late afternoon without them, to help your circadian rhythm understand the full extent of the day.

✓ **Meditation/Mindfulness:** Practising mindfulness has been shown to enable our sleep. Some popular apps, such as Headspace or Calm, have guided meditations specifically related to sleep.

✓ **Increase vitamin D intake:** Some studies have found evidence that problems sleeping can be caused by vitamin D deficiency. Common sources of vitamin D include salmon, tuna, and cod liver oil, and supplements can also be taken.

✓ **Reduce caffeine and (eliminate) alcohol intake:** As mentioned before, if you must drink caffeine, drink it in the morning. Alcohol consumption at night is typically the culprit behind interrupted, poor-quality sleep. The best medical advice is abstinence, but failing that, reduce alcohol intake as much as possible.

✓ **Chart your progress**: Find your personal formula for a good night's sleep by tracking your daily sleep against that day's behaviours (use this checklist as a guide), so you can repeat behaviours that help you sleep better and cut back on those that disturb you.

✓ **Create a comfortable sleeping environment:** Clean, fresh linen and a cool temperature can make a big difference in getting us in the mood to sleep. Ideal room temperature for sleep should be roughly 18.5 C (a lot lower than most of us are used to), but it is easier to sleep in a cold room than a warm room, as that more closely mirrors our drop in body temperature, signalling to the body that it is time to sleep.

During the evening:

✓ **Turn down the lights sooner:** Our exposure to light, especially LED light sources such as mobile phones and laptops, interferes with our levels of melatonin (the hormone that governs our sleep patterns).

✓ **Set up a bedtime routine:** Many people find that a warm shower or bath works well as part of this, as the immediate drop in body temperature following the bath/shower signals sleep time to the body – being conscious about your routine over time can help you identify what works for you.

✓ **Incorporate gratitude and savouring rituals in your daily routine:** Deliberate expressions of gratitude (e.g. keeping a gratitude journal) and savouring activities boost our positive emotion – and positive emotions have been positively associated with sleep quality.

During the night:

✓ **Avoid catastrophic thoughts about not getting enough sleep:** Although sleeping well is preferable, we *can* function okay the next day even on limited sleep when required. You may want to consider having a notebook on your nightstand where you can write down any worry that wakes you in the night, so you can 'solve' it in the morning and take it out of your brain by putting it onto the paper. This symbolic act can liberate you temporarily, so you can fall back asleep.

✓ **Sleeping in segments may be natural:** Research studies have found that when unnatural light is removed from our environment, we often sleep in segments. In between segments, we can meditate, be social and undertake other activities, before going back to sleep. So if you wake up in the middle of the night, this may just be your body's natural cycle.

✓**Use sleeping aids if necessary:** For evolutionary reasons, some background noise (e.g. the crackling of a fire) can put us at ease and make it easier to fall asleep. If you are having trouble sleeping in total silence, playing a recording of these sounds may help.

✓**What is your rhythm?** Research has shown that roughly 40% of people are 'morning people' – their natural circadian rhythm wakes them earlier and they are able to go to sleep earlier too. Thirty per cent of people are 'evening types' who naturally prefer going to bed late and waking late. The remaining 30% lie somewhere in the middle, with a slight leaning towards evening types. Identifying your natural preference and adapting to that wherever possible, could also save frustration and do your body and mind a lot of good.

Exercise XIV: Resilient Lifestyle Check

Take the time to read and reflect:

Meditation	Exercise	Diet	Sleep
Meditation increases density of brain tissue, regulates hippocampus, releases serotonin, GABA, melatonin, lowers cortisol levels	Exercise generates endorphins, reduces cortisol levels, and keeps our muscles and organs healthy	Meets basic brain/body reward needs, and thus impacts biological and cognitive performance	Sleep is the body's way to get rid of toxins, hardwire learning, rest the mind and body, and thus impacts biological and cognitive performance

Self-Reflection: Which of these am I already doing? Which can I do more of? Which can I incorporate as low-hanging fruit? Which can I modify for marginal gains?

How does this apply to your child?

Whilst children may not take to so much information at a young age, simple awareness of the advantages of breathing and sitting still for a bit (meditation), eating healthily (diet), loving sports (exercise), and getting enough nightly sleep, should be enough to plant the right seeds.

Funnily enough, young children are brilliant at living in the moment and focusing on the now, so this is one area where we can look to them as teachers and guides. 'Not losing that inner child' becomes a more powerful statement when we understand this. One of my favourite quotes, which some attribute to Albert Einstein, is 'There are only two ways to live your life. One is as though nothing is a miracle. The other is as though everything is a miracle'. That sense of wonder, curiosity, and engaging mindfully and fluidly in activities which children know how to do so well, could help us adults transition from living more mindfully to later learning how to apply that focus onto meditative practices.

That said, children will copy what they see. If you eat junk food but extol the advantages of eating salads, your children are unlikely to mimic the healthy habit, at least in the short term. If you do not exercise or do not join in on their exercise fun, then it is unlikely they will be inspired to do that in the short term either. So the first way for this to seep into your child's lifestyle is to work it into your own.

Did you know that by the time a female in the UK reaches fifteen, her likelihood of engaging in sixty minutes of moderate activity per day falls to 41%? With rising evidence that 50% of mental health illnesses occur before this age, keeping an eye on our levels of physical exercise is a crucial way to prevent such episodes in our children.

In the UK, NHS statistics reported that students from Years 1-13 spent less than two hours a week participating in physical activity. It is a real disservice to students, as scientists have growing evidence to show that, as well as elevating the quantity of serotonin, norepinephrine and dopamine in the brain, activity participation can help us rewire our brain, preparing our minds to better absorb information.[37] Selecting your child's school with the knowledge of how much physical education is included, and

---

[37] Ratey, 2008.

finding alternative ways to round this out for your child is the key to ensuring they build the right level of physical habits to sustain the benefits of sufficient motor activity, enhancing the likelihood they will develop a love affair with sport. Most importantly, providing variety in physical activity so that children can find the one they love will be essential for them to develop the intrinsic motivation to play that sport, so as to create and sustain a longer-term habit around it (or a shifting form of exercise in later stages of their life).

Perhaps the most important of all is teaching your children the skill to fall asleep as early as possible. As Dr Estivill puts it in *A Dormir Niño*, his book about children's sleep, children are not born knowing how to fall asleep on their own. They need to be taught. They also need to be taught what the right amount of nightly sleep is, and parents may need to become tough enforcers of this, particularly at a young age when children dislike going to bed. Working in partnership with schools, parents should aim to follow NHS guidelines for healthy sleep in kids:

NHS Guidelines for Healthy Sleep

1 year: daytime: 2 hours 30 minutes; night-time: 11 hours

2 years: daytime: 1 hour 30 minutes; night-time: 11 hours 30 minutes

3 years: daytime: 0 to 45 minutes; night-time: 11 hours 30 minutes to 12 hours

4 years: night-time: 11 hours 30 minutes

5 years: night-time: 11 hours

6 years: night-time: 10 hours 45 minutes

7 years: night-time: 10 hours 30 minutes

8 years: night-time: 10 hours 15 minutes

9 years: night-time: 10 hours

10 years: night-time: 9 hours 45 minutes

11 years: night-time: 9 hours 30 minutes

12 years: night-time: 9 hours 15 minutes

13 years: night-time: 9 hours 15 minutes

14 years: night-time: 9 hours

15 years: night-time: 9 hours

16 years: night-time: 9 hours

What if you've not established healthy sleeping routines yet? Do not despair! The guidelines we provided above for adults go just as well for children. In fact, most child sleep experts extol the advantages of a nice evening routine. So working in partnership with your child to discover the right routine could become a joint problem-solving exercise that helps to engage their inner detective and creative mind, and build their self-efficacy, whilst doing something wonderful for themselves.

Exercise XV: Children's Resilient Lifestyle Check

Take the time to re-read and reflect on the following:

Meditation	Exercise	Diet	Sleep
Meditation increases density of brain tissue, regulates hippocampus, releases serotonin, GABA, melatonin, lowers cortisol levels	Exercise generates endorphins, reduces cortisol levels, and keeps our muscles and organs healthy	Meets basic brain/body reward needs, and thus impacts biological and cognitive performance	Sleep is the body's way to get rid of toxins, hardwire learning, rest the mind and body, and thus impacts biological and cognitive performance

Self-Reflection: Which of the above could you help your child embed into their routine?

At the right time, discuss the importance of MEDS with your child and ask them what they think. Then ask them which category they'd like to do better in and how they can do so. Just asking them to think through this on their own will empower them to do more of this in the future.

Next Level:

If you need help to teach your children meditation (and for you to dabble in it too), following are some other suggestions besides the apps *Headspace* and *Calm*:

1) *Sitting Still Like a Frog* – this easy-to-read book comes with a CD that features meditations for your children

2) Christiane Kerr's guided meditations and visualisations for kids – we found these to be particularly useful for when one of our kids struggles to fall asleep due to worries

3) Yoga Pretzels activity cards to engage in fun-filled breathing and yoga exercises as a family

A note on yoga

To close out this chapter, I wouldn't be true to myself if I didn't highlight the usefulness of one of my favourite activities of all time – yoga. You need not be flexible to practise yoga. You need not be a yogi, or highly spiritual, or strong, or calm. Yoga asana – meditation in movement – is a wonderful way to tackle all four of the MEDS framework. It is a great exercise and an easy way to dabble in meditation/mindfulness, the advantages of the latter being that over time the quality of our sleep enhances, and even our anxiety related to food can disappear.

Although this need not be you, once you dabble in yogasana and start engaging in meditation, you may also find that it starts to broaden your sense of meaning (PERMAS) if you decide to follow the eight limbs of yoga. Yoga can also help you generate more positive emotions (PERMAS), by allowing you to build feelings of contentment and tranquillity. It can help you develop engagement (PERMAS) through the focus and flow you experience once you have been practising for a while. Furthermore, it can help you build relationships (PERMAS) within the yoga community and, given the lower levels of anxiety you will experience, it will also help you develop patience to deal with people differently. It may even allow you to develop a feeling of accomplishment (PERMAS), as you see yourself improve and create more space in your body, attaining postures you never thought would be possible. Most importantly, it will help you develop self-acceptance (PERMAS), as you learn to accept your natural limitations.

But I digress, as this book is based on the scientific research behind human flourishing. We already mentioned some of the work that Buddhist monks have been conducting in partnership with neuroscientists to get to the bottom of why meditation is so good for you. Yogis practise meditation by virtue of engaging in yoga asana and the ending practise of Savasana – the final posture in any yoga class. Savasana translates as corpse pose in Sanskrit, and its aim is to lay still flat on your back and keep your mind blank or focused on your breath – a short meditation, if you will. Yogis also practise various types of breathing techniques called pranayama. The scientific benefits of these breathing exercises have been well documented now, and practices such as Sophrology, or the democratisation of 'counting to ten', attest to the fact that they work.

If the evidence above is not enough, allow me to tell you how my personal relationship to yoga evolved, and why I attribute so much of my ability to flourish after the passing of both my parents to it.

I discovered yoga at nineteen, after my mother was diagnosed with cancer. During her final months classes became my haven of tranquility and a place to put my brain on 'hold'. Yoga gave me strength, patience, and a way to battle what would have otherwise been extreme anxiety and depression after her passing. I practised hot yoga for years, because of how physically challenged I felt, and the many mental benefits I derived, including increased concentration, enhanced efficiency, and high levels of energy. The practice kept me fit for years to follow. Then, after delivering my first baby and hyperextending my back, I got injured. Through physio sessions to strengthen my core, I grew more aware of my body and my need to not just use flexibility but also strength to stay safe. I turned to running, weights, and other types of strength classes to keep me going, but I made little time for exercise as I resumed my global executive career while simultaneously juggling two young kids.

It wasn't until my father passed away in 2014 that I found my way to yoga again, only this time with a focus to go less deeply into postures (learning to drop the ego) and build more strength. I eventually earned my yoga alliance teacher training certification in 2018, which helped me find my happy medium and a daily self-practice (that I can fit into the smallest of hotel rooms, when I'm on the road). I'm grateful to yoga for helping me through my hardest times and making me a stronger, better, and more resilient person. In 2019, I became a children's certified yoga teacher, in order to transmit to my children my love for this practice, and in the hope they will be armed with the tools to help them stay resilient for life. I'm not getting too far there … yet!

Recap: Building Proactive Resilience

✓ Deliberately generating and prolonging positive emotion can boost health, performance and longevity. This is necessary, as we are not evolutionarily wired to naturally focus on the positive.

✓ Positive emotions go beyond happiness to encompass love, joy, gratitude, serenity, interest, hope, pride, amusement, inspiration, and awe.

✓ These emotions play a crucial role in our survival, as when experienced, our brain broadens, becoming more creative, more agile, and better equipped to learn. Experiencing these emotions is also crucial to help us build a buffer of resilience that we can draw upon when times get tough.

✓ When we experience positive emotions, our brain segregates four main 'happy' neurochemicals: oxytocin (released when we feel we belong), serotonin (released when we feel mastery), dopamine (released when we obtain something we crave), endorphins (released when we push ourselves beyond our pain threshold). We can use knowledge of these neurochemicals to power our performance.

✓ Savouring is the act of prolonging positive emotion by anticipating the event, being mindfully present during the event, and reminiscing about the event. Try including this in your family routine to help your child do the same.

✓ How we react to others' good news is a huge predictor of relationship quality. The next time your child tells you good news, go beyond congratulating them and invite them to savour the news by asking questions about how they found out and how it made them feel.

✓ Expressions of gratitude such as keeping a journal of things that we are grateful for has been shown to reduce symptoms of anxiety and feelings associated with depression. Find ways to include more gratitude into your life and inspire your child to do the same.

✓ Identifying and using our strengths daily can help us reach a state of flow, where we are fully immersed in a highly enjoyable activity. This helps us feel mastery, and can power our performance, as well as lift the performance of those around us. Actively strengths-spot within yourself, your child, and those around you to create a thriving environment, by articulating precisely what the strength is.

✓ Turn a praise into an opportunity to make you and your child consciously competent, by describing the specific action taken, and how that affected others for the better. This will not only develop a feeling of mastery and engagement, but it will also give meaning to actions.

✓ Incorporate **M**editation, **E**xercise, **D**iet, **S**leep into your life and family routine.

Conclusion Beyond Succeeding to Thriving

This book has attempted to guide you through a deliberate approach to building resilience, presenting leading research from positive psychology, neuroscience, and the C-suite to help you and your child lead a flourishing life. We've covered the importance of aligning our life and goals to our intrinsic motivation, and how teaching our children to set, work towards, and celebrate milestones towards the achievement of smaller goals can help them do the same once they identify their life goals. We discussed how building a growth mindset and stress-is-enhancing mindset, and knowing more about our basic needs and what happens when those requirements are unmet, can help us power our performance, allowing our brains to become more agile and adaptable. We later learned and applied tools to build reactive resilience by changing our explanatory style when bad events happen, separating bad events from our feelings to understand that controlling our thoughts can change our mood and thus actions, and finding ways to turn bad days around through the use of reset buttons. Finally, we discussed how proactively generating positive emotion, and all the techniques to do so, can help us lead a sustainably flourishing life.

So now that you've managed to get your head around all the context and skills in this book, how does it all come together?

Have I come any closer to convincing you that deliberately developing your child's resilience by focusing on your child thriving and flourishing, as opposed to enabling their path to traditional 'success', is the right way to go? For those that still need a little nudge, that still believe if their child doesn't make CEO, they aren't setting them up for the good life, let me share some insights from the leadership advisory space for you. I selected this field as opposed to athletics, the arts, or other fields, merely because of my experience in it, and because the sector has devoted a substantial amount of time and money analysing what leads to success within it.

Scholastic success is typically predicted with a traditional IQ test, albeit there are now more forward-thinking institutions, which are applying the theory of multiple intelligences instead. However, the educational system is still predominantly guided by defining success as someone who scores well on tests and performs well against predetermined milestones. Yet, leadership advisory firms, companies dedicated to finding, assessing, placing and in some cases helping to develop C-suite executives through coaching or advisory interventions, have specific elements that they look for in future leaders, and IQ plays only a small role. Different firms have different models, but most agree IQ is just one of many other attributes that predict executive 'success'.

Some firms focus on learning agility, and others have specific potential models they have developed. Some take it one step further and argue IQ is just a traditional measure of verbal and quantitate reasoning, which isn't that relevant in the workplace, and they have developed their own measurement for executive intelligence. For the purposes of dissecting how this is all relevant to our discussion around resilience from an early age, let's use Egon Zehnder's publicly available model of potential. This defines leadership potential by the presence of four attributes:[38] intellectual curiosity, insight, engagement, and determination. Interestingly, most children are born with these attributes and it is up to us parents to, at minimum, not hinder their growth, and at

---

[38] Fernández-Aráoz, 2014.

best, foment these skills. By building resilience, as outlined in this book, your child will *sustain* the potential to flourish to the highest level of their chosen endeavour.

Intellectual Curiosity

This attribute drives people to proactively seek understanding through gathering new information, experiences, and ideas. Children are naturally curious. You may recall, or be in the midst of the 'why' phase – where every other word is followed by an inquisitive 'why'. Every child uses this sense of wonder to learn to interact with the world, walk, talk, and play. They learn to fail fast and repeatedly, and keep exploring to understand the world around them long before they have the words to voice their curiosity.

This is closely linked to children's ability to later derive meaning. Those who are encouraged to keep asking why, whose curiosity is rewarded with knowledge, a smile (even after the umpteenth time), or a gentle 'we will discuss this tomorrow when we wake up' that is later followed up on, are more likely to continue to use that neural circuit well into adulthood. They can then ask themselves the big questions and align their lower-level goals to their higher-level ones, sustaining persistence of motive towards their chosen destination.

Determination

This trait, shared across all high performers, enables the ability to reach desired goals through razor focus. Determined individuals enjoy a challenge and overcome obstacles; they commit to a goal and learn how to self-regulate to get there. Goal alignment is just one way to achieve it, and developing a growth mindset is another to ensure the failures along the way energise us to keep going. That said, every child has it in them. Have you observed a child learning to crawl or walk? You may recall their frustration, crying, and interludes of giving up or losing interest ... but every child who is physically able will eventually learn how to walk. They have grit within them.

Children who are supported, given tools and encouragement

to keep trying, and whose failures are celebrated with a supportive smile, will find the energy and inspiration to keep going. Children whose parents, educators, and primary caretakers instil a growth mindset, an understanding of stress mindset, and insights into their neural workings, will be better equipped to pick themselves up when they fall. Those who learn to use ABC and have knowledge of their cognitive distortions will be able to course-correct when setbacks inevitably arise. This neural circuit can be developed and serve them well into adulthood when they have to push just that little bit harder to reach their higher-level goals.

Engagement

This attribute is the ability to win the hearts and minds of those around us and galvanise them towards a desired action. This trait allows people to connect with others, and it usually manifests because they are driven to get to know others at a deeper level. Their energy and enthusiasm are contagious, and can thus inspire others to act and follow. Find a smiling baby and watch the effects on adults around it – people just start to smile and engage with it in the most natural of ways. Babies have innate charming abilities, which is evolution's way of making sure we don't abandon them during those challenging first months and years, when their dependency can make our lives that much harder. Babies haven't built mental scripts about what it means to be 'naughty' or what it means to be 'successful'. All these labels, definitions, cognitive short cuts, results of experiences and language used around them, can later become cognitive distortions and points of reference that are hardwired as they grow up.

Encouraging children to problem-solve empathically, as described in the Aligning Life and Mindset sections; encouraging them to use ABC tools to find alternative explanations for people's behaviours; and helping them understand how their own brain works when feeling 'left out' or 'unsafe', will arm them to maintain healthy, strong relationships. Children who are taught active constructive responding will develop stronger altruistic joy circuits, demonstrate more empathy, and develop longer-lasting relationships. Children who are taught about the advantages of using strengths, will also be able to spot those around them and undoubtedly find many people that will want to follow them, because they will make others feel good. Indeed, children taught to have an optimistic explanatory style and to take care of their mental and physical well-being through MEDS, will be sources of joy and positivity for those around them. Deploy the skills in this book and you will be helping your child develop interpersonal and intrapersonal relationships that they can use to foment their ability to engage others, as well as the world around them.

Insight

Insight is the ability to process a range of information from many sources, put disparate pieces of information together, and come up with a different way of thinking. It can also be the ability to digest deeply complex pieces of information and make them simple. Imagine coming into this world with a relatively blank canvass and learning to walk, talk, and engage in less than eighteen months! Every brain has the ability to learn, and every brain has the ability to connect the dots. It is true, some of us are naturally born with higher levels of 'processing power' than others, but as we discussed earlier, the brain is plastic and it can learn and grow. Embracing a growth mindset and intellectual curiosity will inevitably enhance the likelihood that our children can develop this attribute further. Encouraging the *Whole-Brain Child* approach in Drs Bryson and Siegel's book, described in this book in the context of connecting the upstairs, downstairs and left and right parts of the brain, will go a long way in supercharging whatever intellectual horsepower your child is born with. Remember, as Daniel Goleman and Richard J. Davidson argued, and leadership advisory work demonstrates, EQ has a much higher impact on long-term success (and this model supports it by devoting three out of the four attributes to it). When the brain's primary needs of safety, belonging, and mastery are met, it is in responsive state, at its most agile. Helping your child recognise this, and self-regulate to ensure they give themselves the best chance to stay in 'responsive' mode for as often as possible, is yet another way to enhance their capabilities.

I hope that by giving you an insight into the world of leadership advisory firms, you can see that the skills that propel someone's career can also be developed if we focus on helping our children flourish rather than focus on the traditional routes to help them just 'succeed' – which often, in spite of our best efforts, can add unnecessary mental health pressures.

Allowing your child to find their true passion, what intrinsically motivates them; helping them learn to set goals and align them to activities they intrinsically value; recognising that their brain can grow; that they can cope with (and thrive under) stress; that they can choose how they react to setbacks and events; that being kind, grateful, and prolonging positive emotions, will not only help them reach flow, but also inspire others. All of these skills will help your child flourish. Flourishing and resilience skills will not only help your child 'succeed' in their chosen endeavours, but also be the best version of themselves, by reaching their ambitions whilst being mindful of their needs so as to not compromise their mental health along the way. Most importantly, these skills will empower them to know they can manage their moods, and that they can ask for help if they need it because they know what a good and a bad mental/physical state feels like. They will have the skills to self-regulate and the language to ask for help where they are unable to do it on their own.

What better gift to give your child than the tools to face the unknowns of their future? Forget getting them into Oxbridge or an Ivy League, or working for Google or Goldman Sachs, becoming business tycoons or heads of state. Our aim should be to help them build resilience to face the world and carve their own paths – whatever they may look like. That outdated blueprint for success may be where they *want* to go, and if so, by all means embrace it. But let's remember that this should not be at the cost of their childhood, or well-being. Hopefully, this book will give you confidence that taking the road less travelled will help mould the best version of your child – whatever that version turns out to be. And if that isn't a lofty parenting objective, then I don't know what is.

The trick is to teach them to identify what they're innately driven by; that they have the skills to align their activities to their overall goal; and to develop the tools to build strong relationships, surmount obstacles, and not be afraid to learn and fail along the way; to savour the great moments, inspiring those around them to do the same, whilst taking care of their physical and mental needs. I am sure you will agree that will make them not just happy human beings, but good ones to get to know also – women and men of virtue and character.

Flourishing people, may you know one, may you be one, may you raise one...

Afterword

Now that you've read the book and hopefully started putting some of these tools into action, take a moment to reflect, and maybe write down below, on a scale of one to ten, how present are these in your life? And your child's?

Positive Emotions		
Engagement		
Relationships		
Meaning		
Accomplishment		
Self-Acceptance		

I hope this book has inspired you to reflect on your personal drivers and behaviours, and that you feel ready to implement some of the changes suggested within your family to guide your child along the path to resilience. Mindsets can be rewired and habits transformed at any stage of life, but to give your child the best chance to thrive, it helps to start young. My company,

3VERS, creates workshops, coaching journeys, and family advisory sessions to help you acquire the knowledge, reflect on how to apply it to your specific situation, and set you on the path to create new habits that will last you and your child a lifetime. We hope you will join us in developing resilient, healthy, confident, flourishing children so we can eradicate the mental health crisis our society faces today.

I'd love to hear from you if you have any questions, or if you'd like to share any changes you've experienced as a result of reading this book. Please feel free to contact me on the details below.

Belen del Amo Perez de Lara, September 2019
Website: www.3vers.com
Email: belen@3vers.com

Acknowledgements

Alone we can do so little, together we can do so much.

Writing this book has been a cathartic process of putting pen to paper, and capturing and giving meaning to my life. *How to Thrive by Building Resilience* is a true culmination of the multitude of people and places that have impacted me in so many ways, making it practically impossible to name them all. (I tell my children to never use the word 'never' and 'impossible', yet here I am!) The friends I made and the teachers I learnt from in the many places I lived—Aberdeen, Great Yarmouth, Litchfield, Comodoro Rivadavia, Mendoza, Cutralcó, Neuquén, Buenos Aires, Paris, Mexico D.F., Houston, Dallas, Philadelphia, Padova, Milan, Florence, Menorca, Fontainebleau, Singapore, and London—were instrumental in shaping the person I am today. There were two people, however, that masterfully crafted the foundations and core of who I have become. I have already dedicated the book to them, but I could not end it without mentioning my mother and father yet again. While they may never get the chance to read this, it brings tears to my eyes to know that they are alive through the words in this book, and that when my children read this as they are older, they will continue to live on through them.

I would also like to thank my children, who have taught me more than I could have ever imagined. They taught me to rekindle my love of just being; to appreciate the little moments. To see life as a miracle, experiencing things that seemed ordinary as if for the first time. They helped me ask myself all the tough questions, which, if left unanswered, would have meant I led a less meaningful life. They helped me develop patience and derive further inspiration to become a better person day in, day out. Through their personal experiences, they inspired me to think how the work I do with executives can help children, and planted the seed that there may be room for a book like this to help others. Most importantly, they are a source of joy. I have no idea what they will become when they grow up, but I have faith they will be incredible human beings that will pursue happiness and take pleasure in helping others do the same. I already see that in them.

Although expressing my gratitude to my husband publicly will probably make him blush, I must do so anyway. There are too many things to thank him for, but if forced to pick one reason, it is because he sees in me what I do not see in myself, and accepts me just as I am. He has taught me to love myself, and continues to be a source of inspiration for me, as I aim to be as comfortable in my own skin as he is in his. He has proven a wonderful partner in the lifelong project of raising our two children. If it weren't for him, I wouldn't have had the confidence to put pen to paper, and certainly wouldn't have had the family that allowed me to draw such inspiration in the first place.

I am so grateful to my Perez Fitzgerald Co-founder, Simon Flynn, who introduced me to the world of positive psychology, and without whom I may have never embarked upon an entrepreneurial career. He was instrumental in helping me get to grips with the vast world of research in this budding field, and helped craft a number of exercises peppered throughout the book that once targeted the executive audience.

Thank you so much to my friends Ana Queipo, Nandini Basuthakur, Myrto Gouti, Alexandra Cochrane, Florence Assant, Sara Kesserwani, Laura Coffey, Sandra Schwarzer, Lamees Al-Ashtal, and Raffaele Turco. Your feedback during the early stages of the manuscript helped me crystallise my thoughts and improve the manuscript, and gave me confidence to keep going when I struggled to believe in myself. To Yasmine Bekkari, Lili Fortin and Kerry Ghize, your friendship over the years has not only helped me be kinder to myself and become more self-aware, but it was also instrumental in developing a number of tools that I share in the book today. You all know I do not use the word 'friend' lightly, and you have each touched my life in so many different ways.

My heartfelt gratitude and admiration go to Jo Wallace, Head Teacher at Kensington Wade, for leading the school to become the first UK institution to embrace the 3VERS Resilience Journeys for Educators. The amazing staff at the school that participated in the sessions not only helped me improve the teachings, but also taught me so much about what great teachers do on a daily basis. My hat goes off to you and all the educators out there who are already teaching our children these skills, against all odds. I will be eternally grateful to you all for helping our daughter and her classmates grow up in such a caring and thoughtful ecosystem.

I'd like to thank Caroline Bell, Steve Kelner, and my other EZ and OPP colleagues for introducing me to the world of executive assessment and psychometric testing, and sharing your knowledge with me so generously and effectively. I enjoyed our partnership and the way it naturally evolved over time, and look forward to our paths continuing to cross.

I would also like to thank my editor, Bryony Sutherland. She was a delight to work with from beginning to end and truly helped me find my voice as a writer. She did more than edit a manuscript: she helped me believe my voice mattered, and that this book could in fact make a positive impact.

To Caroline Goldsmith, for making the words and images in the book shine through as brilliantly as possible and for helping me create a cover that truly embodies the essence of the book. Her wealth of knowledge in the industry has been priceless and I could have not completed the last leg of this journey without her help.

To Patricia de Semir for the beautiful picture that graces the cover of this book. It encapsulates resilience through a picture of our children climbing into the unknown, propelled by the love of family and armed with the confidence that they can surmount any obstacle that comes their way. The cover image of this book is a reflection of her talent.

I cannot end the acknowledgements without mentioning Dr Maria Isaac. She helped me get back on my feet when I embarked upon the journey of pregnancy without a mother. She taught me that my parent's teachings were inside me, and that I merely needed to look inside to find my inner guide. She also armed me with powerful tools that sustained my mental health through challenging times. She has become more than a mentor, and I truly consider her my friend. Besides the comfort she gave me of the scientific rigour in this book, she gifted me with the most beautiful of realisations: if one day, my children write a paragraph about me that remotely resembles what I write about my mother in this book, then I can die a happy and fulfilled human being. What greater gift than to know I have transmitted the love my parents gave to me to my children, so they can transmit it to future generations.

Thank you also to YOU for reading this book, and embarking on this journey with me. I hope our paths will cross, and that you feel inspired to embrace the tools that serve you.

Bibliography

Aamodt, Sandra and Wang, Sam (2011). Welcome to Your Child's Brain: From in Utero to Uni. New York, NY: Bloomsbury.

Achor, Shawn (2010). The happiness advantage: The seven principles of positive psychology that fuel success and performance at work. New York, NY: Crown Publishing.

Arden, John B.; PhD. (2010). Rewire Your Brain: Think Your Way to a Better Life. Hoboken, NJ: Wiley & Sons.

Aurelius, Marcus (2006). Meditations. London, UK: Penguin Classics.

Baumeister, Roy F., and Tierney, John (2011). Willpower: Rediscovering the greatest human strength. New York, NY: Penguin Books.

Beck, Aaron T. (1967). Depression: Causes and treatment. Philadelphia, PA: University of Pennsylvania Press.

Beck, Aaron T., Epstein, Norman, and Harrison, Raymond (1983). Cognitions, attitudes and personality dimensions in depression. London: British Journal of Cognitive Psychotherapy.

Begley, Sharon (2007). Train Your Mind, Change Your Brain. New York, NY: Ballantine Books.

Benabou, Roland and Tirole, Jean (2003). Intrinsic and Extrinsic Motivation. Review of Economic Studies 70, 489–520.

Benton, David and Donohue, Rachel T. (1999). The effect of nutrients on mood. Public Health Nutrition, 2(3A): 403-30.

Bernard, Sara (2010). Neuroplasticity: Learning Physically Changes the Brain. Edutopia.org.

Blackwell, Lisa, Trzesniewski Kali, and Dweck, Carol (2007). Implicit Theories of Intelligence Predict Achievement Across an Adolescent Transition: A Longitudinal Study and an Intervention. Child Development. doi: 10.1111/j. 1467-8624.2007.00995.x.

Brdar, Ingrid and Kashdan, Todd B. (2010). Character strengths and well-being in Croatia: An empirical investigation of structure and correlates. Journal of Research in Personality, 44, 151-154.

Britton, Kathryn (2007). Positive Core and Strengths at Work. Positive Psychology News.

Brown, Nicholas J. L., Sokal, Alan D., and Friedman, Harris L. (2013). The complex dynamics of wishful thinking: The critical positivity ratio. American Psychologist, doi:10.1037/a0032850.

Brown, Tim (2009). Change By Design. London, UK: Harper Collins UK.

Bryant, Fred B. (1989). A Four-Factor Model of Perceived Control: Avoiding, Coping, Obtaining, and Savoring. Journal of Personality 57(4):773-797.

Bryant, Fred B., Smart, Colette M. and King, Scott P (2005). Using the Past to Enhance the Present: Boosting Happiness Through Positive Reminiscence. Journal of Happiness Studies, v6, i3, 227-260.

Bryant, Fred B., and Veroff, Joseph (2007). Savoring: A new model of positive experience. Mahwah, NJ: Lawrence Erlbaum.

Bryant, Fred B., Chadwick, Erica D., and Kluwe, Katharina (2011). Understanding the processes that regulate positive emotional experience: Unsolved problems and future directions for theory and research on savouring. International Journal of Well-being, 1(1), 107-126. doi:10.5502/ijw.v1i1.18.

Burnham, David and McClelland, David C. (2003). Power Is the Great Motivator. Boston, MA: Harvard Business Review.

Burns M.D., David (1999). Feeling Good: The New Mood Therapy. New York, NY: Harper Collins.

Buschor, Claudia, Proyer, René T., and Ruch, Willibald (2013). Self- and peer-rated character strengths: How do they relate to satisfaction with life and orientations to happiness? Journal of Positive Psychology, 8 (2), 116-127.

Butler, Andrew C. and Beck, J. S. (2000). Cognitive therapy outcomes: A review of meta-analyses. Journal of the Norwegian Psychological Association, 37, 1-9.

Cialdini, Robert (2017). Pre-Suasion: A Revolutionary Way to Influence and Persuade. London, UK: Random House Business.

Clifton, Donald O., and Harter, James K. (2003). Investing in strengths. K. S. Cameron, J. E. Dutton, and R. E. Quinn (Eds.), Positive organizational scholarship (111-121). San Francisco, CA: Berrett-Koehler.

Corporate Leadership Council. (2004). Driving performance and retention through employee engagement. Washington, DC: Corporate Executive Board.

Coyle, Daniel (2009). The Talent Code: Greatness isn't born. It's grown. Here's how. London, UK: Random House.

Crabb, Shane (2011). The use of coaching principles to foster employee engagement. The Coaching Psychologist, 7(1), 27-34.

Crum, Alia J., and Langer, Ellen J. (2007). Mind-set matters: Exercise and the placebo effect. Psychological Science 18, no. 2: 165-171.

Crum, Alia J., Corbin, William R., Brownell, Kelly D., and Salovey, Peter (2011). Mind over milkshakes: Mindsets, not just nutrients, determine ghrelin response. Health Psychology, 30(4), 424-429.

Csikszentmihalyi, Mihaly (2002). Flow: The classic work on how to achieve happiness. London, UK: Random House.

Cyrulnik, Boris (2011). Resilience: How Your Inner Strength Can Set You Free from the Past. London, UK: Penguin Books.

Dietrich, Arne (2004). Neurocognitive mechanisms underlying the experience of flow. Conscious and Cognition. Dec;13(4):746-61.

Dobson, Keith S. and Block, L. (1988). Historical and philosophical bases of cognitive behavioral theories. Handbook of Cognitive behavioral Therapies. Guilford Press, London.

Duckworth, Angela (2016). Grit: The Power of Passion and Perseverance. New York, NY: Scribner Book Company.

Dunn, Linnea (2017). Lagom: The Swedish Art of Balanced Living. London, UK: Gaia Books.

Dweck, Dr Carol (2007). The Perils and Promises of Praise. Educational Leadership, v65, n2, p34-39, October 2007.

Dweck, Dr Carol (2006). Mindset: The New Technology of Success. London, UK: Constable & Robinson.

Dweck, Dr Carol (2010). Even Geniuses Work Hard. Educational Leadership, v68 n1 p16-20.

Dubreuil, Philippe, Forest, Jacques, and Courcy, François. (2013). From strengths use to work performance: The role of harmonious passion, subjective vitality and concentration. Journal of Positive Psychology. DOI:http://dx.doi.org/10.1080/17439760.2014.898318.

Duhigg, Charles (2012). The power of habit: Why we do what we do in life and business. New York, NY: Random House.

Condry, John and Chambers, James (1978). Intrinsic Motivation and the Process of Learning. M. Lepper and D. Greene (eds.) The Hidden Cost of Reward: New Perspectives on the Psychology of Human Motivation, Hoboken, NJ: Wiley & Sons.

Dalai Lama (1999). The Art of Happiness: A Handbook for Living. London, UK: Hodder Paperbacks.

Eagleman, David (2015). The Brain: The Story of You. Edinburgh, SCO: Canongate Books.

Edmonds, Caroline J. and Burford, Denise (2009). Should children drink more water? The effects of drinking water on cognition in children. Appetite, 52(3): 776-9.

Ellis, Albert (1957). Rational Psychotherapy and Individual Psychology. Journal of Individual Psychology, 13: 38-44.

Ellis, Albert (1962). Reason and Emotion in Psychotherapy. New York, NY: Stuart.

Emmons, Robert A. and McCullough Michael E. (2003). Counting blessings versus burdens: An experimental investigation of expressions of gratitude and subjective well-being in daily life. Journal of Personality and Social Psychology.

Estivill, Eduard (2016). A Dormir Niño (translated into English as 'Five Days to a Perfect Night's Sleep'). Barcelona, SP: Debolsillo.

Fernández-Aráoz, Claudio (2009). Great People Decisions: Why They Matter So Much, Why They are So Hard, and How You Can Master Them._Hoboken, NJ: Wiley & Sons.

Fernández-Aráoz, Claudio (2014). 21st-Century Talent Spotting. Boston, MA: Harvard Business Review, June 2014 issue.

Fernández-Aráoz, Claudio (2014). Boston, MA: Harvard Business Review Press.

Fredrickson, Barbara L. (1998). What good are positive emotions? Review of General Psychology, 2, 300–319. doi: 10.1037/1089-2680.2.3.300.

Fredrickson, Barbara L. (2001). The role of positive emotions in positive psychology: The broaden-and-build theory of positive emotions. American Psychologist, 56, 218–226. doi: 10.1037/0003-066X.56.3.218.

Fredrickson, Barbara L. (2009). Positivity. New York, NY: Crown.

Fredrickson, Barbara L. (2013). Updated Thinking on Positivity Ratios. American Psychologist. Advance online publication. doi: 10.1037/a0033584.

Fredrickson, Barbara L. (2013). Love 2.0. New York, NY: Random House.

Fredrickson, Barbara L. (2013). Positive emotions broaden and build. P. Devine and A. Plant (Eds.), Advances in experimental social psychology (Vol. 47, pp. 1–54). San Diego, CA: Academic Press.

Fredrickson, Barbara L., and Joiner, Thomas. (2002). Positive emotions. C. R. Snyder and S. J. Lopez (Eds.), Handbook of positive psychology (pp. 120–134). Oxford, UK: Oxford University Press.

Fredrickson, Barbara L., and Losada, Marcial F. (2005). Positive affect and the complex dynamics of human flourishing. American Psychologist, 60(7), 678–686. doi: 10.1037/0003-066X.60.7.678.

Fredrickson, Barbara L., Cohn, Michael A., Coffey, Kimberly A., Pek, Jolynn, and Finkel, Sandra M. (2008). Open hearts build lives: Positive emotions, induced through loving-kindness meditation, build consequential personal resources. Journal of Personality and Social Psychology, 95, 1045–1062. doi: 10.1037/a0013262.

Gable, Shelly L., Reis, Harry T., and Downey, Geraldine (2003). He said, she said: A quasi-signal detection analysis of daily interactions between close relationship partners. Psychological Science, 14(2), 100-105.

Gable, Shelly L., Reis, Harry T., Impett, Emily A., and Asher, Evan R. (2004). What do you do when things go right? The intrapersonal and interpersonal benefits of sharing positive events. Journal of personality and social psychology, 87(2), 228.

Gable, Shelly L., Gonzaga, Gian C., and Strachman, Amy (2006). Will you be there for me when things go right? Supportive responses to positive event disclosures. Journal of personality and social psychology, 91(5), 904.

Gallup. (2013a). Gallup-Healthways Well-Being Index 2013. Retrieved from http://info.healthways.com/wbi2013.

Gallup. (2013a). State of the American workplace. Retrieved August 24, 2014, from http://www.gallup.com/strategicconsulting/163007/state-american- workplace.aspx.

Gallup. (2013c). The State of the global workplace: Employee engagement insights for business leaders worldwide. Retrieved August 24, 2014, from http://www.gallup.com/strategicconsulting/164735/state-global-workplace.aspx.

Gander, Fabian, Proyer, René. T., Ruch, Willibald, and Wyss, Tobias (2012). The good character at work: An initial study on the contribution of character strengths in identifying healthy and unhealthy work-related behaviour and experience patterns. International Archives of Occupational and Environmental Health, 85(8), 895-904.

Garcia, Hector and Miralles, Francesc (2017). Ikigai: The Japanese Secret to a Long and Happy Life. London, UK: Hutchinson.

Gardner, Howard E. (2006). Multiple Intelligences: New Horizons in Theory and Practice. Basic Books.

Gardner, Howard E. (2011). The Unschooled Mind: How Children Think and How Schools Should Teach. New York, NY: Basic Books.

Gladwell, Malcolm (2008). Outliers: Stories of Success. London, UK: Penguin Books.

Goleman, Daniel and Davidson, Richard J. (2017). Altered Traits: Science Reveals How Meditation Changes your Mind, Brain and Body. New York, NY: Avery Publishing Group.

Gominak, Stasha and Stumpf, Walter E. (2012). The world epidemic of sleep disorders is linked to vitamin D deficiency. Journal: Medical Hypothesis.

Govindji, Reena, and Linley, Alex P. (2007). Strengths use, self-concordance and well-being: Implications for strengths coaching and coaching psychologists. International Coaching Psychology Review, 2 (2), 143-153.

Graham, Tyler and Ramsey, Drew, MD (2011) The Happiness Diet: A Nutritional Prescription for a Sharp Brain, Balanced Mood, and Lean, Energized Body. New York, NY: Rodale Books.

Graybiel, Ann. M. (1998). The basal ganglia and chunking of action repertoires. Neurobiology of learning and memory, 70(1), 119-136.

Graziano Breuning, Loretta, Carlin, Amanda et al. (2017). Habits of a Happy Brain: Retrain Your Brain to Boost Your Serotonin, Dopamine, Oxytocin, Endorphin Levels. London, UK: Adams Media.

Gruber, June, Quoidbach, Jordi, Mikolajczak, Moïra, Kogan, Alexsandr, Kotsou, Ilios and Norton, Michael I. (2014). Emodiversity and the Emotional Ecosystem. Journal of Experimental Psychology: General, Vol. 143, No. 6, 2057–2066.

Hanson, Rick and Mendius, Richard (2009). Buddha's Brain: The Practical Neuroscience of Happiness, Love and Wisdom. Oakland, CA: New Harbinger.

Hanson, Rick (2013). Hardwiring Happiness: The Practical Science of Reshaping Your Brain – and Your Life. London, UK: Rider Books.

Harter, James K., Schmidt, Frank L., and Hayes, Theodore L. (2002). Business unit-level relationship between employee satisfaction, employee engagement, and business outcomes: A meta-analysis. Journal of Applied Psychology, 87, 268–279.

Harter, James K., Schmidt, Frank L. and Keyes, Corey L. M. (2003). Well-being in the workplace and its relationship to business outcomes: A review of the Gallup studies. C. L. Keyes and J. Haidt (Eds.), Flourishing: Positive psychology and the life well-lived (pp. 205-224), Washington, D.C.: American Psychological Association.

Harzer, Claudia, and Ruch, Willibald (2012). When the job is a calling: The role of applying one's signature strengths at work. The Journal of Positive Psychology, 7(5), 362-371.

Harzer, Claudia, and Ruch, Willibald (2013). The application of signature character strengths and positive experiences at work. Journal of Happiness Studies, 14(3), 965-983.

Harzer, Claudia, and Ruch, Willibald (2014). The role of character strengths for task performance, job dedication, interpersonal facilitation, and organizational support. Human Performance, 27(3), 183-205.

Heath, Chip and Heath, Dan (2007). Made to Stick: Why some ideas take hold and others come unstuck. New York, NY: Random House.

Heath, Chip and Heath, Dan (2010). Switch: How to Change Things When Change is Hard. New York, NY: Crown Business.

Heaversedge, Dr Jonty and Halliwell, Ed (2010). The Mindful Manifesto: How doing less and noticing more can help us thrive in a stressed-out world. London, UK: Hay House.

Hefferon, Kate (2013). Positive Psychology and the Body: The somatopsychic side to flourishing. London, UK: Open University Press.

Hodges, Timothy D., and Harter, James K. (2005). The quest for strengths: A review of the theory and research underlying the StrengthsQuest program for students. Educational HORIZONS, 83, 190-201.

Hodges, Timothy D., and Asplund, Jim (2010). Strengths development in the workplace. In A. Linley, S. Harrington, and N. Garcea (Eds.), Oxford handbook of positive psychology and work (pp. 213–220). Oxford, UK: Oxford University Press.

Horesh, Netta and Apter, Aalan (2006). Self-disclosure, depression, anxiety, and suicidal behaviour in adolescent psychiatric inpatients. Crisis: The Journal of Crisis Intervention and Suicide Prevention, 27(2), 66-71.

Hurley, Daniel B. and Kwon, Paul (2012). Results of a Study to Increase Savouring the Moment: Differential Impact on Positive and Negative Outcomes. Journal of Happiness Studies – J HAPPINESS STUD. 13. 10.1007/s10902-011-9280-8.

Irvine, William B. (2009). A Guide to the Good Life: The Ancient Art of Stoic Joy. Oxford, UK: Oxford University Press.

Jackson, Todd, Soderlind, Adam, Weiss, Karen E. (2000). Personality traits and quality of relationships as predictors of future loneliness among American college students. Social Behaviour and Personality and International Journal, Vol 28, 463-470.

Jamieson, Jeremy P., Berry Mendes, Wendy, Blackstock, Erin, Schmader, Toni (2010). Turning the knots in your stomach into bows: Reappraising arousal improves performance on the GRE. Journal of Experimental Social Psychology 46(1): 208-212.

Jensen, Frances E.; M.D. and Nutt, Amy Ellis (2015). The Teenage Brain. London, UK: Harper Paperbacks.

Kirschenbaum, Daniel S., Ordman, Arnold M., Tomarken, Andrew J., and Holtzbauer, Robert (1982). Effects of differential self-monitoring and level of mastery on sports performance: Brain power bowling. Cognitive Therapy and Research, 6(3), 335-341.

Klein, Gary (1998). Sources of Power: How People Make Decisions. Boston, MA: MIT Press.

Kramer, Roderick M. (2003). The Harder They Fall. Boston, MA: Harvard Business Review, October 2003.

Kruglanski, Arie W., Shah, James Y., Fishbach, Ayelet, Friedman, Ron, Chun, Woo Young and Sleeth-Keppler, David (2002). A Theory of Goal Systems. Advances in Experimental Psychology.

Lee, Julia J., Gino, Francesca, Cable, Daniel M. and Staats, Bradley (2016). Preparing the Self for Team Entry: How Relational Affirmation Improves Team Performance. Boston, MA: Harvard Business School, Working Paper, No. 16-111, March 2016.

Linley, P. Alex and Joseph, Stephen (2004). Positive Psychology in Practice. Hoboken, NJ: Wiley & Sons.

Little, Brian R. (2011). Me, Myself and Us: The Science of Personality and the Art of Well-being. New York, NY: PublicAffairs.

Littman-Ovadia, Dr Hadassah, and Steger, Michael (2010). Character strengths and well-being among volunteers and employees: Toward an integrative model. The Journal of Positive Psychology, 5(6), 419-430.

Littman-Ovadia, Dr Hadassah, and Davidovitch, Dr Nitza (2010). Effects of congruence and character-strength deployment on work adjustment and well-being. International Journal of Business and Social Science, 1(3), 138-146.

Lyubomirsky, Sonja (2010). The How of Happiness: A Practical Guide to Getting the Life You Want. London, UK: Piatkus.

Masten, Ann S., Cutuli, J.J., Herbers, Janette E. and Reed, Mair-Gabrielle J. (2009). Resilience in Development. In C. R. Snyder, and S. J. Lopez (Eds.), The handbook of positive psychology (2nd Edition ed., pp. 117-131). Oxford, UK: Oxford University Press.

Menkes, Justin (2005). Hiring for Smarts. Boston, MA: Harvard Business Review, November 2005.

Minhas, Gurpal. (2010). Developing realized and unrealized strengths: Implications for engagement, self-esteem, life satisfaction and well-being. Assessment and Development Matters, 2, 12-16.

Mitchell, Joanna, Stanimirovic, Rosanna, Klein, Britt, and Vella-Brodrick, Dianne (2009). A randomised controlled trial of a self-guided internet intervention promoting well-being. Computers. Human Behavior, 25(3), 749-760.

Mogi, Ken (2017). The Little Book of Ikigai: The Secret Japanese Way to Live a Happy and Long Life. London, UK: Quercus Books.

Morgan, Nicola (2013). Blame My Brain: The Amazing Teenage Brain Revealed. London, UK: Walker Books.

Neal, David T., Wood, Wendy, and Quinn, Jeffrey M. (2006). Habits—A repeat performance. Current Directions in Psychological Science, 15(4), 198-202.

Park, Nansook, Peterson, Christopher, and Seligman, Martin E. P. (2004). Strengths of character and well-being. Journal of social and Clinical Psychology, 23(5), 603-619.

Park, Nansook, and Peterson, Christopher (2009). Character strengths: Research and practice. Journal of College and Character, 10 (4), 1-10.

Pearson, Dr Ian (2016). Society Tomorrow: Growing older in 21st Century Britain. CreateSpace Independent Publishing Platform.

Peterson, Christopher. (2000). The future of optimism. American Psychologist, 55(1), 44-55. http://dx.doi.org/10.1037/0003-066X.55.1.44.

Peterson, Christopher and Seligman, Martin. (2004). Strengths of Character and Well-Being. Journal of Social and Clinical Psychology – J SOC CLIN PSYCHOL. 23. 603-619. 10.1521/jscp.23.5.603.50748.

Peterson, Christopher (2006). A Primer in Positive Psychology. Oxford, UK: Oxford University Press.

Peterson, Christopher, Stephens, John Paul, Park, Nansook, Lee, Fiona, and Seligman, Martin E. P. (2010). Strengths of character and work. In Linley, A., Harrington, S., and Garcea, N. (Eds.). Oxford handbook of positive psychology and work (pp. 221-231). Oxford, UK: Oxford University Press.

Plassmann, Hilke, O'Doherty, John, Shiv, Baba and Rangel, Antonio (2008). Marketing actions can modulate neural representations of experienced pleasantness in PNAS January 22, 2008 105 (3) 1050-1054.

Pollay, David J. (2007). Gratitude and Giving Will Lead to Your Success. Positive Psychology News.

Pollock, David C. and Van Reken, Ruth E. (2009). Third Culture Kids: Growing Up Among Worlds. London, UK: Nicholas Brealey Publishing.

Proyer, René. T., Gander, Fabian, Wyss, Tobias, and Ruch, Willibald (2011). The relation of character strengths to past, present, and future life satisfaction among German–speaking women. Applied Psychology: Health and Well–Being, 3(3), 370-384.

Proyer, René. T., Ruch, Willibald and Buschor, Claudia (2012). Testing strengths-based interventions: A preliminary study on the effectiveness of a program targeting curiosity, gratitude, hope, humor, and zest for enhancing life satisfaction. Journal of Happiness Studies, 14(1), 275-292.

Proyer, René. T., Gander, Fabian, Wellenzohn, Sara, and Ruch, Willibald (2013). What good are character strengths beyond subjective well-being? The contribution of the good character on self-reported health-oriented behavior, physical fitness, and the subjective health status. The Journal of Positive Psychology, 8(3), 222-232.

Ratey, John and Manning, Richard (2014). Go Wild: Free Your Body and Mind from the Afflictions of Civilisation. London, UK: Little, Brown.

Rath, Tom (2007). Strengths Finder 2.0. Washington, DC: Gallup Press.

Rath, Tom and Harter, Jim; Ph.D (2010). Well-being: The five essential elements. Washington, DC: Gallup Press.

Rath, Tom (2013) Wall Street Journal. How to Improve (and Increase) Your Sleep.

http://blogs.wsj.com/speakeasy/2013/12/19/how-to-improve-and-increase-your-sleep/

Reivich, Karen (2003). The Resilience Factor: 7 Keys to Finding Your Inner Strength and Overcoming Life's Hurdles. New York, NY: Broadway Books.

Rimm, David.C. and Litvak, Stuart. B. (1969). Self-verbalization and emotional arousal. Journal of Abnormal Psychology, 74(2), 181.

Robinson, Michael D. and Moeller, Sara K (2014). Frustrated, but not flustered: The benefits of hierarchical approach motivation to weathering daily frustrations. Motivation and Emotion.

Robinson, Sir Ken (2010). The Element: How Finding Your Passion Changes Everything. London, UK: Penguin Books.

Roffey, Sue. (ed.) (2012). Positive relationships: Evidence-based practice across the world. New York, NY: Springer.

Ryan, Richard M. and Deci, Edward L. (2000). Intrinsic and Extrinsic Motivations: Classic Definitions and New Directions. Contemporary Educational Psychology, 25 (54- 67).

Seligman, Martin (1998). Learned Optimism: How to Change Your Mind and Your Life. New York, NY: Vintage Books.

Seligman, Martin (2002). Authentic Happiness: Using the New Positive Psychology to Realise Your Potential for Lasting Fulfilment. London, UK: Nicholas Brealey Publishing.

Seligman, Martin, Steen, Tracy A., Park, Nansook, and Peterson, Christopher. (2005). Positive psychology progress: Empirical validation of interventions. American Psychologist, 60, 410–421.

Seligman, Martin (2007). The Optimistic Child: A Proven Program to Safeguard Children Against Depression and Build Lifelong Resilience. Boston, MA: HMH Books.

Seligman, Martin (2011). Flourish: A New Understanding of Happiness, Well-being and How to Achieve Them. London, UK: Nicholas Brealey Publishing.

Shepard, Lorrie A. (1979). Self-Acceptance: The Evaluative Component of the Self-Concept Construct. American Education Research Journal, V16, n2. P. 139-160.

Siegel, Dr Daniel J. and Payne Bryson, Dr Tina (2012). The Whole-Brain Child: 12 Proven Strategies to Nurture Your Child's Developing Mind. UK: Constable & Robinson.

Sofi, Fransesco., Cesari, Francesca., Abbate, Rosanna., Gensini, Gian Franco and Casini, Alessandro. (2008). Adherence to Mediterranean diet and health status: meta-analysis. British Medical Journal, 337: a1344.

Spreier, Scott W., Fontaine, Mary H. and Malloy, Ruth L. (2006). Leadership Run Amok. Boston, MA: Harvard Business Review, June 2006 Issue.

Sternberg, Robert. J. (1984). Toward a triarchic theory of human intelligence. Behavioural and Brain Sciences, 7, 269–287.

Sternberg, Robert. J. (1985). Beyond IQ: A triarchic theory of human intelligence. Cambridge, UK: Cambridge University Press.

Sternberg, Robert. J. (1997). Successful intelligence. New York, NY: Plume.

Sternberg, Robert. J. (1999). The theory of successful intelligence. Review of General Psychology, 3, 292–316.

Sternberg, Robert. J. (2003). Wisdom, intelligence, and creativity synthesized. Cambridge, UK: Cambridge University Press.

Sternberg, Robert. J. (2011). The theory of successful intelligence. In R J. Sternberg and S. B. Kaufman (Eds.), Cambridge handbook of intelligence (pp. 504-527). Cambridge, UK: Cambridge University Press.

Peters, Dr Steve (2012). The Chimp Paradox: The Mind Management Programme for Confidence, Success and Happiness. London, UK: Vermilion.

Peters, Dr Steve (2018). My Hidden Chimp. London, UK: Studio Press.

Stewart, Abigail (1982). Motivation and society. San Francisco, CA: Jossey-Bass Inc Publishing.

Thaler, Richard H. and Sunstein, Cass. R. (2009). Nudge: Improving decisions about health, wealth, and happiness. New York, NY: Gildan Media, LLC.

Walker, Matthew (2017). Why We Sleep. London, UK: Penguin Books.

Wiking, Meik (2016). The Little Book of Hygge: The Danish Way to Live Well. London, UK: Penguin Books.

Wiking, Meik (2018). The Little Book of Lykke: The Danish Search for the World's Happiest People. London, UK: Penguin Books.

Wood, Alex M., Linley, P Alex, Maltby, John, Kashdan, Todd B., and Hurling, Robert (2010). Using personal and psychological strengths leads to increases in well-being over time: A longitudinal study and the development of the strengths use questionnaire. Personality and Individual Differences, 50, 15-19.

Wrzesniewski, Amy, McCauley, Clark, Rozin, Paul, and Schwartz, Barry (1997). Jobs, careers, and callings: People's relations to their work. Journal of Research in Personality, 31(1), 21-33.

About the Author

Belen del Amo Perez de Lara is a Scottish-born Spaniard. As an only child, raised all around the world, she lived in more than twenty-one cities across four continents by the age of twenty-four. Having to rebuild her life year on year, she was faced with the loss of both her parents to cancer during key periods of her life. She used these life experiences and her professional career to codify a process, shared in this book, that helped her and others thrive in the best and worst of times.

Belen graduated from the University of Pennsylvania with a triple major, Summa Cum Laude and Phi Beta Kappa. She obtained her MS from LSE and an MBA from INSEAD. She started her career at JP Morgan, Accenture, then led commercial teams at CEB (now Gartner). After obtaining her fully funded MBA, she joined Egon Zehnder, one of the world's top leadership advisory firms, where she specialised in the assessment of C-suite executives. Headhunted to build the Talent Management Function at George Soros' philanthropy, Open Society Foundations, she eventually became Global Head of HR, Security and Facilities.

After her father passed away, Belen co-founded Perez Fitzgerald to help executives, teams, and organisations build resilience. In 2018, she launched 3VERS, to additionally help parents and educators develop resilience in themselves and their children. Belen is a certified yoga teacher by the Yoga Alliance, a member of the British Psychological Association, has published case studies with CESEDEN (the Spanish Ministry of Defence's think tank) and INSEAD's Global Leadership Centre, and routinely challenges herself with new experiences – her latest one was training for and running her first (and last) marathon in Stockholm. She speaks Italian, French, Spanish, and English, and lives with her husband and two children between London and Menorca.

Printed in Great Britain
by Amazon

35501915R00121